In Spite of the System

A Personal Story of

Wrongful Conviction

& Exoneration

Gary Gauger with Julie Von Bergen

Fourcatfarm Press   ◆   Lake Geneva, Wisconsin

In Spite of the System: A Personal Story of Wrongful
Conviction and Exoneration

ISBN 13: 978-0-9791452-0-9
Library of Congress Control Number: 2008923209

Designer: Charisse Antonopoulos

Printed in the United States of America
13 12 11 10 09 08   6 5 4 3 2 1

Fourcatfarm Press, Lake Geneva, Wisconsin 53147

Contents

For my sister, Ginger

You CANNOT CONCEAL the confusion you feel
as they steadily work to out-guess you.
And some will pretend they are really your friend
who rally around to your rescue.
With frightening force your mind is divorced
to give them the guilty impression.
Every word that you hear is a weapon of fear
to win the war of confessions.

from
"The Confession"
by Phil Ochs

Farewells and Fantasies, 1997

Preface

I CRINGE INWARDLY EVERY TIME I catch myself describing what Gary Gauger endured as a "good story." But that's exactly what I first thought when I reread the details of his ordeal after he was pardoned by former Illinois Gov. George Ryan in 2002. That may be your reaction, too, even if you're already familiar with Gary's case.

But as you read Gary's first-person book, keep in mind that his story is not unique. People are regularly arrested, convicted, and even executed for crimes they didn't commit. It took an extraordinary set of circumstances and a dedicated group of people to free Gary and clear his name. Others aren't so fortunate.

Some wonderful people helped bring Gary's book to life. Nicola Nelson is at the top of the list. She allowed us to use the personal letters Gary wrote to her from the McHenry County Jail and Stateville Prison. Her generous spirit is characteristic of many of the people in Gary's circle of friends.

A big thank you goes to Marilyn Magowan and Kathy Freund, who shared their office space with me and allowed me to work in peace and quiet. Without their help, my family would have had to step over piles of court documents, newspaper clippings, and letters in the early days of this project.

My whole family, especially my husband, Ed, has been very supportive of me and this book. It has been part of our lives for more than five years. Lynn Greene and Linda Godfrey, my good friends and fellow writers, were always on hand to lend their mavenly encouragement.

Sue Gauger comes last, but certainly not least, on this list. I think Gary would be the first to admit that without her, I might still be waiting for him to find old family photos or court documents. She is the true coeditor of this book.

If you'd like to learn more about Gary, his story, and the death penalty, please visit his website at www.garygauger.com. We will post information on Gary's speaking schedule, updates on his case, and resource links.

Julie Von Bergen
May 2008
Lake Geneva, Wisconsin

CHAPTER 1

Thursday Morning

◆ APRIL 8, 1993

I HIT THE ALARM BUTTON and went back to sleep. Five in the morning was early for me. Even on a clear day in early April the sun didn't rise in northern Illinois until nearly six thirty, and at that hour, the dim light of my unfinished greenhouse didn't provide enough illumination for the delicate work of transplanting seedlings from their nursery beds to the cold frames and hot beds just outside the building. Today it was raining, and even darker.

As I slept, James Schneider—known as Preacher to other members of the Outlaws motorcycle gang—left Lake Geneva, Wisconsin, about fifteen miles away from our farm, and picked up Randall "Madman" Miller at his Pell Lake home a few miles south. There was little traffic on Highway 12 as they drove to the Illinois border; just the usual early morning parade of pickup trucks on their way to factories and job sites, or office workers on autopilot as they headed to Fox Lake to catch an early commuter train to Chicago. At Genoa City the four-lane highway narrowed before it entered Richmond, the small Illinois village where I grew up.

Our farm is about three and a half miles east of town on Highway 173, a two-lane road lined with farms and an occasional business. The area was still overwhelmingly rural in 1993, but its location on the northwestern edge of the Chicago metropolitan area was starting to show signs that Richmond would soon be another exurban enclave of subdivisions of big houses on big lots.

Schneider turned left on 173 and the two Outlaws headed for our farm. About a mile down the road, he pulled over to switch

The Gauger family

The Gauger farm near Richmond, Illinois.

license plates on their car. Schneider and Miller were on their way to rob and murder my parents, and they didn't want to take any chances.

Miller reminded his friend of the goal. "They've got to have about $30,000 in that house," he said. "I want to have the people separate. I don't want to kill them both together."

I woke again, this time to the sound of rain beating on my window. No sense worrying about transplanting, since I couldn't go outside. My parents, Ruth and Morrie, were certainly already up. They began their days early, a habit from their days as active farmers. Although they were now semiretired, there was plenty to do around the farm. My dad ran a motorcycle repair shop in a garage just behind the house, and my mom helped my sister, Ginger, sell the rugs, blankets, and artifacts she brought back from her trips abroad. My dad was seventy-four and opened the shop officially only two or three days a week. Even so, there would always be a slow but steady flow of regular customers stopping by to talk bikes, see what was new, or to pick up an occasional part for some vintage motorcycle.

My mom would usually be finishing her morning chores at this hour or already be about her business, running errands or helping my dad in the shop.

This morning, my dad was out back feeding the chickens, part of his regular morning routine. My mom stayed in the kitchen, finishing a cup of coffee and planning her day. There was a knock at the door.

"Where's the youngster?" Miller asked, smiling at my mom. Figuring he was one of my dad's motorcycle customers, she told him that Morrie was out back, and Miller headed that way.

Schneider, playing his own part, told my mom he'd like to take a look at Ginger's rugs in the trailer. "I want to pick out a present for my girlfriend, since I'm here," he said. My mother led the way through the wet yard and unlocked the little padlock that secured the trailer. As soon as she stepped in, Schneider pulled a gun out of his back pocket and hit her twice on the back of the head. She fell to the ground, making a little moaning noise. He tucked the gun back in his pocket and pulled out a knife, then lifted her up by her hair and cut her throat from ear to ear, watching as her blood gushed out. He covered her body with some of Ginger's blankets, left the trailer, and snapped the padlock again.

Schneider made his way to the back of the house to find Miller, who was standing outside the motorcycle shop. Schneider silently signaled to Miller that he had taken care of my mother, and the two went into the shop to confront my dad. They didn't waste time on small talk. "We want your money, Morrie. We know you got money here," Miller said. "We were here before and found the bag with the thousand dollars in it. Give us the money, Morrie. We've got your wife locked up."

My dad held out a little dish containing a small amount of cash. Miller knocked it to the ground and repeated his demand, louder this time. "This is a robbery. A R-O-B-B-E-R-Y," he yelled. He pulled out his gun and pointed it at my dad's head, pushing him around the shop's service counter and into the back room. Schneider heard a sound like someone being hit and a body falling to the ground, then the gurgling, raspy sound of my dad trying to breathe with his throat cut.

Miller stepped back into the main room of the shop and confirmed that he had killed Morrie. He also told Schneider he had decided to stab my dad in the side with his knife, just to see how it felt going in. "Like a knife in butter," he reported.

They picked the money up off the shop floor, swearing when they discovered the total was no more than fifteen dollars. Schneider was nervous about leaving evidence, even though he and Miller had worn gloves and put their hair in hairnets under their hats before they got to the farm. Miller was a bit more confident they had taken proper precautions, but even so they didn't look around the shop for more money or go in the house to see what was there. If they had, I have no doubt they would have killed me, too.

Instead, they left. They put the license plates in the front and back windows of their car and pulled out onto 173. Back on Highway 12, they turned off almost immediately at a rest stop in Genoa City and washed the blood off their knives in a puddle before continuing to Lake Geneva, where they stopped for breakfast at the Olympic Restaurant on Main Street. Miller ate heartily, joking that he could kill a person and eat spaghetti with extra red sauce right afterwards. Schneider, more squeamish about what had just happened, stuck with chocolate milk. They paid the tab with the little money they netted from the robbery.

I woke again to the sound of the rain lashing against the east wall of my bedroom. By now the early morning light was just starting to filter through the cloudy plastic that still covered the inside of my window as protection against the winter chills that invaded the poorly insulated farmhouse.

I tried to get up, but my limbs and mind still felt drugged with sleep. I'd been sober for five weeks, but my body was still throwing off the effects of twenty years of recurrent alcohol and marijuana abuse. Winter is my off season, and months of staying up, feeding the shop fire, cranking up the radio, and slamming twelve-packs of Budweiser took its toll.

I hit the TV "on" button, hoping to catch the weather on the *Today* show. After trying for half an hour to stay awake long enough to hear the local forecast, I turned it off, resigned to the fact that the rain was going to be around for a while.

———

MILLER AND SCHNEIDER drove to Lake Como, a small, shallow lake a few miles north of Lake Geneva. They dumped their knives and gloves in the murky water and later burned everything they had worn that morning.

EIGHT FORTY-FIVE A.M. This time I was awake for good, ready for a full day's transplanting and blessed with a perfectly cloudy day to do it on, if the rain let up. It was a meditative job that needed to be repeated many times in the next eight weeks to get my 15,000 pepper and tomato plants ready for direct placement in the fields.

I got up.

CHAPTER

2

The Quiet House

THE HOUSE WAS UNUSUALLY QUIET as I walked through it just before nine o'clock that morning. Even though my parents were often out for the day by this time, something didn't feel quite right. I had a feeling in my gut that reminded me of the sensation I sometimes had after waking from a night of heavy drinking. That and the empty feeling of the house made me look in places my mom would have left a note if they had gone away. I thought perhaps they had gone on a trip with their friend Windy to Sugar Grove, Illinois, to look at some old bikes and tractors. The day trip had been planned for the previous week, but had been put off because my dad was getting over the flu.

I'd lost half a day of work Tuesday getting parts for an old Super M tractor I was rebuilding. I think my dad wanted to show me the tractor boneyard up past Whitewater, Wisconsin, as much as anything, so my parents and I made the trip in mom's little Ford Escort. We could have bought what I needed for fifty bucks from a local tractor dealer, but that wasn't my dad's way.

The old tractor graveyard was well worth the trip and we got everything we went for. We also stopped at my brother Gregg's house in Whitewater and talked to him for a while. Little did I realize it would be my last outing with my folks.

I had gone to bed early Wednesday night. My dad, still easily tired from his illness, decided to make it an early evening, too. Although my mom said she wasn't feeling too well either, she decided to stay up a little longer. In the days that followed, I sometimes wondered if she was worried about something.

When I walked into the kitchen, I saw Fluffy, one of our cats, on his perch outside the door. He was wet and looked extremely crabby, like he'd been out there for some time waiting to be let in. Usually if my mom was going away, she'd at least make an attempt to see that the cats got back in on such a nasty morning.

I let him in, made a sandwich, and looked around the kitchen for a note, but they hadn't left one. I noticed some dirty dishes in the sink and a coffee stain on the stove. I figured they were already up and had already eaten breakfast. My mother was either out helping my dad find parts or had run to town.

But that odd feeling was still nagging me. The house had been burgled a little more than a year before after we'd all left on a Sunday to watch an antique tractor show. Someone had gone through the entire house but had only taken some money from Ginger's rug business and a few old coins from my father's dresser. The fact that they took so little led me to believe that whoever was responsible had walked up the lane and seized the opportunity to steal on impulse. Otherwise, some of Ginger's more valuable rugs and my dad's guns and motorcycle parts would have been gone.

I recalled that burglary now because when we got back home that night, another of our cats, Tousie, had still been terrified and visibly shaken. I looked at him closely now to see if anything seemed wrong. He was a little surprised by the close attention, but not at all upset. I gave his pal Fluffy a pat on the head on the way out the door and took a close look at him, too. Things also seemed normal with him, so I brushed off the feeling, went out the back door, and walked around to the driveway.

I looked down the lane to see if the gate was up or down. When the shop was closed, we stretched a chain across the driveway where it met Route 173. I couldn't see if the chain was halfway or all the way across the driveway, but at this time of day, either position would be normal. Since I was already late and the rain had let up, I hurried across the field to my greenhouse, eager to get to work.

A typical day for me would be to start a fire in the woodstove for heat (both for me and my plants), put some coffee water on, turn on the radio, roll a small joint, and smoke part of it while I settled in, listened to *The Steve and Garry Show* on WLUP, and planned out my day.

On days I did smoke, I would never smoke more than one small joint of "homegrown," and that would be over the course of the whole day. Spring is my busy time of year and I just didn't have time for such nonsense. In the afternoon, I would usually take my version of a three thirty break — high tea, the old joke goes — and smoke a little more. In the evening, I'd crank up the shop radio, take a couple of hits, and do evening projects.

The day was actually a little warmer than I expected and the rain had stopped, so I started transplanting right away rather than going through my morning ritual. I had most of the plants out of the greenhouse already and wanted to set the rest out before the rain started again.

I got a good jump on transplanting and finally made the coffee about forty minutes later. I could see I'd be done in an hour or so, so I sat down and lit a joint, enjoying the light rock in the background.

Gene Lyp and his nephew, Gary, came by a little later. We looked over Gene's Triumph, then talked about his nephew's bike — he had taken a spill and wanted my dad or me to get it back into shape. They told me they had stopped at my folks' before heading to my greenhouse, but said everything was locked up.

I didn't realize he had been up to the house itself. I should have asked. I'd have realized the gate was down and probably would have gone back to put it up and check around to make sure nothing was missing or wrong. If I had, I may have realized much earlier that my folks had not, in fact, gone to Sugar Grove.

After Gene and Gary left, Art Kauke, a local farmer who rented a barn from my dad, stopped in. We exchanged our usual rural salutations and talked about bikes a little. Then he got to the point of his visit. "Remember you said you'd help me move a pig today?" he asked. It was time for a female to have a little visit with the male.

Art and I work together like Mr. Ziffel and Newt Kiley of *Green Acres*. When I was drinking, I'd often go out to the barn to shoot the breeze with Art while he took care of his pigs. I'm sure he thought I was pretty strange, but the pigs liked me because I was generous with apples. They'd hear my voice and sixty snouts would be right there at the boards.

But Art and I knew how to get the job done. I usually ask the pig politely if she'd mind coming out and moving down a few pens for her date. Art always thinks that's very funny, but the mature pigs know the routine. So with no visible urging, she's out of the pen, down the walkway, and in with the boar.

After Art left, I continued to work at the greenhouse until six thirty, the time I usually had dinner with my parents at the house. I walked the 400 yards back to meet them there, figuring by then that they'd be back from wherever they had been. I went in the back door, which was always unlocked, and saw no evidence of anyone being home that day. I checked their bedroom and saw that the bed wasn't made.

If they had left early to go on a trip, it wasn't unheard of for my mom not to make the bed. She wasn't compulsive about it. Still, the unmade bed and the lack of a note—and the fact that they weren't home at six thirty—*did* worry me.

Rather than stay home alone and worry, I ate supper and went back to the greenhouse to finish an order for some spring supplies I still needed. When I left the house, I checked the door to my dad's shop. It was locked, another indication no one was home. I worked at the greenhouse until ten, then walked back home.

Now that it was dark, I noticed for the first time that one light was on in the middle parts room of the garage that served as my dad's shop. That's how they would have left things if they were going away just for the day and planned to come back after dark. It was supposed to create the illusion that someone was around. *Reader's Digest* had published an article about how burglars look for this, and it was a family joke. The Burglar Beacon: We didn't want a burglar to trip on something and sue us.

I looked in the window but saw nothing. If my father had been in the garage, a light would be on in the back room where he worked, and the front door would be open. The back room was dark and the door was locked.

I reassured myself that there was probably no note because they figured they'd be back before I got home. We generally went about our own business during the day and often didn't see each other until dinnertime.

When my father had a minor stroke two years before, my mother followed the ambulance in her car. So I went out to the barn to look for her Escort. Still there. All three of my parents' cars were where they should have been, again reinforcing the idea they had left with Windy. He had a new truck, so I wasn't really worried about them breaking down. If there had been an accident, I figured someone would call. I also checked the rug trailer out front. Its only door was padlocked.

I thought about calling the police, but knew they wouldn't investigate a missing persons report without someone being gone for twenty-four hours. I didn't know Windy's number, or even his real name. I didn't know exactly where Sugar Grove was, either, and couldn't imagine who I could call there even if I did. Ginger and her husband, Evan, were teaching skiing in New Mexico, and I felt it was too late to call Gregg.

Intellectually, I could explain it away. They were in Sugar Grove. The house was quiet. Everything was locked up. It made perfect sense to me.

Prodigal Son

THE THREE GAUGER KIDS—Gregg, Ginger, and I—had typical rural childhoods of the fifties and early sixties. We could go off for the day without telling our parents where we were going, and everything was fine as long as we were home before dark.

I don't think I was even in grade school yet when the three of us would get up at sunrise, put on hiking boots, and walk all over the woods. We'd go as far as State Line Road, where an old man lived in a house that hadn't been painted in fifty years. He liked to shoot clay pigeons in his dump, and we'd sneak in and collect the shell casings.

My dad's woods are barely recognizable now, but they were the magical places of my childhood. There are three or four freshwater springs, which have always fascinated me. Another favorite spot was where glaciers had deposited ancient fossil boulders dislodged from long-vanished seabeds. My arrowhead hunting ground was in those woods. Once we dug up what the three of us were convinced was an Indian burial mound, but we only found water.

Our family went camping every summer in northern Wisconsin, but once a year my parents would go away together for a few days on their own, usually heading out west on their motorcycles. When my parents were gone on one of their trips, Grandma and Grandpa Gauger would watch us. They lived in a little white house they built on the farm when Gregg was born. The farmstead had been around a lot longer. Grandma and Grandpa bought it in 1923, when the main house was an old roadhouse for Chicagoans on their way to Lake Geneva and points north. The road by our house was only gravel at the time, and Grandpa used to keep the

Photos on this page the Gauger family

Morrie and Ruth on one of their motorcycle trips.

Once a year the Gaugers went on a camping trip together.

horses in harness in the spring to a make a little extra money by pulling people out of the mud.

———

I WAS A BORED KID all through my school years. I daydreamed in class. I went to the woods and creeks instead of doing my home-

Ruth Gauger
with Ginger,
Gregg, and
Gary in the
1950s.

The Gauger family

work and ended up finishing it on the bus in the morning. Somehow I still managed to make pretty good grades.

I started smoking marijuana in my senior year at Richmond-Burton High School, but I managed to keep up a B average. I started drinking a lot earlier. My friends and I would get together and drink until we got sick and passed out.

One night I got picked up for a curfew violation, and the high school principal already knew about it because he met me at the

an easy birth for the baby, too, and she didn't even cry. Just pinked up and looked around, like she was saying, "Here I am." We had visitors just an hour later. I remember being very proud of my wife at that moment.

I was Mr. Mom for a while when Ronda worked, and later, when she was going back to school, I put an addition on our house and took care of the kids.

My wife and I were vegetarian for about seven years. Sometimes into dairy products, sometimes not. I'm completely vegetarian now, but I did eat meat on and off over the years. I always felt that if I were going to use meat as a food source, I should be prepared to kill it. Or at least accept the karma involved in its production.

I've always been into hunting. Not necessarily animals—I prefer hunting mushrooms, arrowheads, wild herbs, and tubers, and I even collected stamps and coins in my earlier years. I was particularly fond of mushroom hunting. It has all the fun and excitement of regular hunting and being out in the woods but without all the violence.

Sometimes when I ate mushrooms I would feel I was literally breathing with the earth. It was like I couldn't even tell where I left off and the air and ground began. To me the mushrooms were always just another herb like tea or coffee. Not really a drug at all.

I used to enjoy Dumpster diving, too. It's a form of recycling, but it's also hunting. Among other things, I found a case of beer; a gallon of laundry soap; thirty pounds of extra sharp Kraft cheddar cheese (still frozen); fifty tubs of yogurt (still cold); forty dollars worth of Little Caesar's pizza pans (the scrap aluminum price); bags of washed, folded clothes; shoes; whole fresh pizzas; and a constant supply of boxes and vegetables. Hitting the Dumpsters was a real adventure for me.

———

ONE OF THE JOBS I had in Texas was with the Internal Revenue Service. People who know me can't imagine me working for the government, but I spent my evenings with someone's 1040 spilled out on my desk like the guts of a newly hit turtle on a busy highway, matching W-2s and 944s with the corresponding data. When people would ask me what exactly I did, I told them I sent bills to widows and orphans, which was true. Of course, we'd send them to other people, too.

My job was to go over three-year-old tax forms that the computer had kicked out because of discrepancies. I'd look at the data, and either clear it, pass it upstairs, or send a bill before the three-year statute of limitations ran out. I did literally thousands of them. I had mixed feelings about the morality of working there, and didn't stay long.

During that period, Ronda would be getting up for class when I got home to go to bed. Then she'd come home and I'd be out the door for work. I hear about other people's marriages, the things they went through, and how they managed to stay together. The only thing I'd do is get sloppy drunk and generally pissed off at the situation I was in. I resented giving up my vegetable business and that Ronda had quit her midwifery practice right away to go back to school. We got married too young and felt trapped before we ever experienced life on our own.

My most satisfying job in Texas was at Austin Community Gardens. The people there were truly dedicated to promoting urban gardening. By the time we arrived the garden organizers had nine sites all over the city and about 250 people rented plots. They were politically organized enough at this point to be able to procure an annual operational budget of around $150,000, a lot of which went to three paid staff members—a full-time director, full-time coordinator, and me, the half-time field manager. The job lasted only one year. Right after I was raised to full time, the recession hit Texas, funds were cut, and the gardens went all-voluntary.

While I was there, I introduced a couple of programs I was proud of, like using the vacant plots to grow row crops for food banking, teaching low-watering techniques, and promoting aggressive composting of the leaves the city picked up instead of sending them to landfills.

As happy as I was working there, it was really a very hard time in my life and the last year of my marriage to Ronda. I discovered Unity Church in Austin right after she filed for divorce. I was going through a bad period and a friend of mine from Alcoholics Anonymous introduced it to me. It was love at first sight. I had developed a negative view toward church and Unity really helped open my eyes. We called it the "church of too much fun." It was a New Age church that embraced the concept of a personal, interactive, and loving relationship with the creator. It had about 1,500 members, and probably that many regular nonmembers. There was something going on all week long, and all day on Sundays. It was a good place to take the kids.

Ronda and I divorced in 1985. It hurt so much to just visit or "date" my kids. But during that time, a friend of mine and a couple of guys he had picked up at the Salvation Army were staying at my house. They were nice people, but everybody was always drinking and smoking pot. It just didn't seem like a place for three young children.

I earned my living selling recycled appliances in Austin until I moved back to Illinois in 1989. I tried to run an honest shop for the benefit of the customers, but I found myself telling white lies (saying my driver's truck broke down, for instance, rather than admit he was probably still in bed smoking dope with his old lady). It got too easy to not be one hundred percent honest all the time, and that's one of the reasons I quit the business.

Organic growing had always been a passion of mine, and I also wanted to reestablish a relationship with my parents. They said I was welcome to move back and help out on the farm. So I left Texas and didn't write to my kids. I was ashamed that I couldn't stop drinking. I had already lost my driver's license. I had no money. I was drinking with the little money that did come in from odd jobs.

It took so long to get the pieces of my life back together—by April 1993 I had been sober for five weeks, the spring farm work was progressing well, my expansion plans were on schedule, and I had lots of bike repair work. I was finally beginning a new chapter of my life.

Friday

FRIDAY MORNING there was still no sign of my parents. Around nine thirty, I noticed a compact car out in the driveway. The driver asked what time the shop would be open, and I told him I didn't know. As we talked, though, it occurred to me that if he had come up the driveway, the gate must be down. After he drove out, I walked down to the road, picked up the newspapers from the past two days and Thursday's mail, then strung the chain across the driveway.

I tried to read the newspaper as I sat by the phone, but my real thoughts were about what to do next. I realized I had to feed the ducks and chickens in the back chicken house, something my dad usually did every morning. As I was going out the door at about eleven, I noticed a couple of people I recognized from the motorcycle shop in the driveway.

I was glad to see Ed Zender and his girlfriend, Traci Fozkos. Ed was in his early twenties, a regular customer, and—despite the age difference—a good friend of my dad's. I told him I hadn't seen my parents since the night before last, and I didn't know where they were.

"Well, I came up here to get some things I need, but in particular I need a nut to keep working on this engine I'm doing," Ed said. "Could you go into the shop and get it?"

"Sure," I replied. The side door was locked, but I knew my dad never locked the overhead door. I rolled it up and climbed over some motorcycle parts to open the door for Ed and Traci. We went back to the mechanic's section and looked through a chest of British nuts and bolts.

"Good eyes, Gary," Traci said when I found some parts that were close. None were an exact match, but Ed was pretty sure the one he needed was with the camshafts in the middle room. I led the way. As we left the brightly lit mechanic's area and made our way into the darker room, I hit my knee on something as I tried to walk down the first aisle, which was supposed to be kept clear. Traci banged her knee, too, and complained that her purse and jacket were getting caught on something sticking out. I couldn't see what the obstruction was, so I cut over to the next aisle and went down that one. The light was a little better there, and by then my eyes were adjusting.

I made a little turn to head for the doorway and stopped short. My dad was there on the step, lying on his side in a pool of blood, his legs tucked up into almost a fetal position. I stepped over him, kneeled down and put my hand on him. His body was stiff and cold, and he didn't have a pulse. On his feet were the rubber boots he wears when he feeds the chickens. "Oh, jeez, Dad," I said.

Ed tried to tell Traci to stay back, but by now she had made her way down the first aisle and was standing behind us. "Is that Morrie?" she said, crying as she reached over to pat my dad's hand.

"He's gone," I finally managed to say. "He must have had a stroke and banged his head. I guess we'll have to call the paramedics. Oh, man, where is my mom?"

My legs were heavy as I tried to stand up. I moved like a sleepwalker. Somehow I managed to get to the house to make the call.

I went back to the garage a few minutes later. Ed had stepped in my dad's blood and tracked it everywhere. I didn't realize there was so much. I said a short prayer over my father's body and whispered, "Dad, I'm very sorry I never told you how much I loved you when you were alive." I went back outside, where Ed and Traci were waiting in the driveway. Shaking, I asked them for a hug, and the three of us just held on to each other for a few seconds.

The paramedics arrived within minutes. I recognized someone I had gone to school with. They rushed past me with their stretchers toward the shop. "There's no reason to hurry," I called out. "My dad is dead. There's nothing you can do."

I went back to check the barn again. I had checked it the night before to make sure my mom's car was there, but this time I wanted to look inside the car itself. There might be something I missed. Ed and Traci went around to the front of the house. I found nothing out of the ordinary and as I came down from the barn, I could see Ed had climbed on the tongue of the trailer, trying without success to see through the window. I didn't go over to look for myself, since I figured I wouldn't be able see any more than he had.

The first police arrived a few minutes later. I gave them permission to search the house, then tried to call my brother. I ended up leaving a message for him with a neighbor. As I was standing by the phone, I found Windy's number and called him. By now I realized there had been no trip to Sugar Grove, of course, but Windy said he hadn't seen my parents at all. I also called my mom's best friend, who lived down the road in Hebron.

After I finished the calls, I did a walk-through of the house with one of the officers, an older man who said he bought a bike from my folks back in the 1960s. "What about the money your dad had on him? It's no secret he carried a lot of cash," he asked when we were upstairs. I asked him what he was getting at and he told me they suspected foul play. I'm sure the police were looking at me right away as a suspect. I was the only person at the scene of the crime, and a family member. But there was no accusing going on, and they didn't treat me like a suspect at first.

Detective Beverly Hendle from the McHenry County Sheriff's Department arrived and asked me to take her through the house. I told her what I had been doing in the last day or so, when I last saw my parents, what my mother was wearing. We walked through the house—upstairs, in the basement, everywhere, looking for my mom.

In court, months later, I was shocked at the absurd things she said about that search. That I stared out the window at the rug trailer, smiled, and said, "You won't find them in the house."

Actually, at that moment we were down in the parlor where Ginger kept her Navajo rugs, looking out the east window. The trailer was out the south window. And since another police officer had just gone through the upstairs, I knew we weren't going to find anyone up there.

––––––––

THE YARD HAD FILLED with police and I stayed outside with them, answering questions as they came up. During a lull in the questions, the sun came out. I told one of the officers I was going next door to the greenhouse for a few minutes to open my cold frame before my tomato plants cooked in the sun. It could happen in a matter of fifteen or twenty minutes and I had two months' work invested in those plants. The officer didn't have a problem with my leaving.

I met Art Kauke and Jerry Hansen at the end of the path between the two farms. Jerry was my dad's best friend and I considered him a friend of mine, too. Another friend, Bob Gustafson, had called him and said there were a lot of police cars at our house, so Jerry came over right away. The police wouldn't let him come up the driveway of the main house so he went next door, where he ran into Art.

"What's going on, Gary? Where's your dad?" he asked.

"Oh, man, Jerry. We found him dead, in the shop," I told them. "It looks like he fell and hit his head, but the police told me they think it might be foul play. My mom's missing, too. We have no idea what happened to her."

Jerry and Art looked as stunned as I felt. They walked back to the greenhouse with me and helped me open my cold frames.

There wasn't much conversation. "I'd better get back now, in case the police have any questions," I said when we finished.

Back at the house, I made another cup of coffee and stood with Ed and Traci in the driveway in case anyone wanted to talk to me. The police asked if I knew where to find the key to the trailer padlock. I looked underneath the kitchen cabinet where my mother kept a bunch of keys, but all of them looked too big. "I can't find the right one," I told the police. "Why don't you just hit it with a hammer and pop it open?"

They got a hammer out of the garage and easily snapped off the little lock. One officer went in, then came back out immediately and motioned to the other cops. Six or seven policemen rushed into the tiny trailer. One of them came back and pointed at me. "Get a hold of him! Don't let him go!"

Two uniformed officers held my arms as they led me to a squad car. They had me put my hands on the car as they patted me down, then locked me in the back seat. There was a cage separating the front and back seats, and the doors had no handles on the inside. About five or six officers stood around the squad car.

I sat in the back of the locked squad for about forty-five minutes, completely numb. Looking back, I probably was in shock. Before long, a police officer opened the side door. "It must be getting hot in there," he said, settling into the front seat of the squad. "They found my mother, didn't they?" I asked the officer, Melvin Hunt. He nodded. I figured my parents must have been killed in a robbery. There was no other explanation. "How could anybody do this for money?" I asked him.

Throughout the afternoon, Hunt followed and kept an eye on me whenever I asked to relieve myself behind a nearby tree. At about three thirty, he got out of the car and spoke to another officer, then poked his head in the door. "We're going to take you to Woodstock," he told me. They transferred me to a marked car, and Detective Hendle joined us again. She repeated that we were going to Woodstock.

"Yeah, I thought so," I said. "Are we going for ridies?"

Sometimes when I'm nervous and uncomfortable I make flippant, stupid comments to try and break the ice. My brother used to tell the dog "we're going for ridies" whenever he'd take him in the car. He got it from a British television program where a dog trainer would say "Walkies!" to cue a dog it was time to go out. It was one of those things that just stuck with our family. Although I didn't realize it at the time, Hendle took my attitude as a sign of guilt.

I got my last glimpse of the farm as we drove west on Highway 173, headed to the McHenry County Sheriff's Department head-quarters about twenty minutes away. Detective Eugene Lowery was waiting for us in an interior interrogation room there. He was a little bull-headed guy with no neck, a crew cut, and a teeny little mustache. Built like a cop. He had the look.

Hendle read me my *Miranda* rights. When they asked if I understood my rights, I said, "¿Qué?," in Spanish. There had just been a big story in the papers about a Hispanic man who won a new trial because he didn't understand English when they read him his rights. I'm sure they were aware of this, but they didn't take the comment as a joke, even though I meant it as one. It was that flip defense mechanism coming out again.

They said they just wanted to ask me some questions. I said I didn't want a lawyer. No, I didn't *need* a lawyer. I was an innocent guy with nothing to hide and I wanted to be eliminated as a suspect as soon as possible so the police would concentrate on looking for the real killer. Then I could go home, talk to Gregg and Ginger, and try to figure out what to do next.

Interrogation

FRIDAY AFTERNOON, FOUR O'CLOCK. I signed a permission form for the cops to search the farm, and the questions started. I went over the details of what I'd done from Wednesday to Friday, even though I'd already told Hendle everything I knew at the farmhouse earlier that day. We went over details repeatedly. I talked about my relationship with my parents and my involvement in Alcoholics Anonymous and the church in Texas.

After a couple of hours, the detectives' conversation, especially Lowery's, became more accusing. Then he switched gears again and began to talk about people who had committed serious crimes and were back on the street. He told me that John Hinckley, who shot Ronald Reagan in 1981, was already free. That didn't seem right, but I figured Lowery would know.

"It's just a matter of working you through the system," he said. "Trust us. You don't want to go to prison. If you cooperate, we can get you into Elgin State Hospital for mental help. If you don't cooperate, we can't help you."

I tried to tell them the house had felt strangely empty, using Counselor Troy from *Star Trek* as an example—in the show, she could grasp the "feel" of a situation. I thought everyone watched *Star Trek*, but apparently Hendle and Lowery didn't. I realized the comparison was going nowhere, so I just stopped talking about the "feel" of the house.

No, my parents didn't have any enemies. No, I couldn't think of anyone who would want to hurt them. I told the detectives someone must have shot them during a robbery. No other theory made any sense at all. Hendle and Lowery said there was a lot of physical evidence left at the crime scene—blood that didn't belong to my parents, and bloody fingerprints by the trailer door. I took this as a positive sign. There were clues.

Friday evening, seven thirty. Lowery wanted to go over some things we'd talked about earlier. I watched him thumb through his notes, which was by this time a rather thick stack of about a dozen pages. Earlier, I had said something along the lines of, "How can somebody face God if they've killed somebody?" and on a page near the bottom of the stack I noticed he had written, in large letters, the words

JESUS FREAK.

I asked him what he meant by that, but he just brushed me off. I didn't have the energy to pursue it. By this time I had completely exhausted the subject of what I had been doing the last three days. I knew less than they did about my parents' deaths.

"I don't know what else I can tell you. Can't we wrap this up so I can go home?" I asked.

"We can't help you if you go, Gary. No, you can't go," he said.

So we kept going over minor points, minute details. I kept thinking that if I could pin down everything I'd done in the last three days down to the precise minute, they'd let me leave.

They kept asking me why I hadn't looked harder for my parents on Thursday night. "A twelve-year-old could do a better job looking for his parents," Lowery said. This made no sense, because I *had* looked around that night, and I told them so. "It doesn't make sense that you and Ed Zender walked up the middle aisle in the garage," he said, even though he knew the first aisle had been obstructed. Lowery got increasingly annoyed that he couldn't get me to change my story. I just looked at him wearily.

"You don't seem concerned about this! You don't show any emotion! I don't get it!" he yelled.

Then they tried a different approach and asked me about my personal life and my relationship with my father. I told them everything I could think of, going back to my earliest memories of my dad. Hendle and Lowery would look at each other, nod, and write something in their notes like I had said something very significant. That kept me going. Maybe there was something crucial in my statements that I didn't recognize.

I told them my life story, everything good and bad I had done since I was a kid. I even mentioned a time more than a decade ago when I put my foot through a wall. That was the most violent thing I had ever done, and I wanted them to realize I could never have killed my parents. Never.

"I have a hard time accepting the fact that you didn't look for your parents, Gary. There are just too many discrepancies. Why did you go up the second aisle, instead of the first?" Lowery repeated the questions over and over. I *had* checked the garage. The door was locked and the light was on. I *had* looked at the trailer. The door was locked from the outside and there was no other way to get in. I just couldn't get them to understand. "There's nothing more I can tell you. Please, can I go home now?" I asked.

Lowery looked at me. "No, you can't. We already told you that. This is your last chance, or we can't help you."

FRIDAY EVENING, TEN THIRTY. I asked if I could take a polygraph test. I couldn't think what else to do. They wouldn't let me go home. I had nothing more I could say. The test would prove I was telling the truth and they'd have to let me go.

The detectives agreed to this suggestion right away. It took about an hour for the Illinois State Police examiner to drive to Woodstock, and while we waited, they brought in some sandwiches. I felt sick and only ate a few bites.

"Is it true some people can practice taking the test and lower their blood pressure?" I asked Lowery as we ate. "I've tried the blood pressure machine at the grocery store and can control my pressure through meditation."

"That doesn't really matter that much," Lowery said. "There are so many aspects to the test, blood pressure is just a small part. We have a lot of faith in these tests. If you pass, we'll all but eliminate you as a suspect."

Friday evening, eleven thirty. Ken Frankenberry, the examiner, asked me to sign a consent form for the test. I also agreed to be videotaped and tape recorded, but nothing came of it. The police led me to another room just down the hall.

Even though it was my suggestion, I was nervous about the test. When Frankenberry walked in and set up the test equipment, I muttered the word "voices," just to see what he would say. Then I realized how strange I must have sounded and told him I didn't mean anything by it. I was just physically uncomfortable and nervous.

"It's entirely normal to be nervous," he said.

Frankenberry started his questions by asking if I knew how my parents were killed. "No, but there was so much blood by my dad's head—they must have been bludgeoned or shot," I said.

He looked at me. "Both had their throats slashed, and your mother's was slashed so severely it almost cut her head off," he said. His words hit me like a fist. What did she go through? Did she know what was happening? Who could have done this?

The test took about an hour. I was exhausted and upset, but I answered truthfully to every question and in the end, figured I had passed with no problem.

Saturday morning, twelve thirty. Lowery was waiting for me in the hall when I left the examination room. "Gary, if you were going to cut somebody's throat, how would you do it?" he asked. I was exhausted and it didn't occur to me to stop and ask why he wanted to know, but I made a motion of grabbing someone's head with my left hand and cutting with my right. "How would you know that?" Lowery pressed. I told him I had seen it done in *Rambo* movies. He didn't say anything more.

I asked him about the test as we walked back to the conference room. "Gary, we can't pass you," he said. Before I could ask how that could be possible, Lowery left and another officer took his place. "Do your parents have a will?" this officer asked. I said I didn't know of one. "It's a shame the estate will go to the state," he continued. "I know that area. Property around there is going for $50,000 an acre." I started arguing about that, then figured he was implying I had killed them for the money. I just stopped talking to him.

Another policeman joined us and asked me a few other unrelated questions, but mostly they just kept an eye on me for about fifteen minutes until Lowery and Hendle returned. "What's this about hearing voices?" she asked right away. "Frankenberry said you said you heard voices."

"He's lying," I said angrily, forgetting the flip comment I'd made an hour and a half earlier.

"No, Gary, he couldn't lie. That would jeopardize his career," she said. Hendle had told me she had worked at the courthouse for thirty years, and had been a detective or police officer for more than twenty. Lowery said he had been a police officer for fourteen or fifteen years. So how could any of them be lying? Why would they jeopardize their careers, everything they had done for so many years?

"Gary," she continued, "do you remember me talking earlier about a stack of evidence we had from the crime scene? What would you say if I told you it was against you?"

"I'd say you're crazy," I told her.

"Well, we do," she said, very sincerely.

Now Lowery started asking me again about what I had done from Wednesday to Friday, demanding to know why I hadn't checked the rug shop or the garage.

I was totally confused. Hadn't we been over this again and again? I *had* checked those places. I *had* seen the rug shop locked. I *had* checked the garage door. I *had* looked in the lighted window of the garage and went to the barn to look for the cars. Yet they kept saying, "You looked everywhere except the places your parents were most apt to be."

SATURDAY MORNING, ONE O'CLOCK. Hendle left and Detective Chris Pandre took her place. He and Lowery went back over the events of Thursday and Friday. "What you're saying makes no sense, Gary," they said, shaking their heads. Then Hendle came back and talked about the evidence they had against me, indicating with her hand that the pile was about five inches thick.

Lowery was almost crying now. "Gary, how could you? How could you kill the woman who gave birth to you? There was no robbery, Gary. No struggle. If it had been a robbery, your parents would have tried to defend themselves. It had to be someone they trusted. Someone who could walk right up to them. And we have the evidence against you, Gary."

I asked them what the evidence was, and they said they couldn't tell me. I asked them when they could tell me, and they said Monday. I didn't know much about police work, but I realized that if it was evidence they could show me in two days, it must be really obvious.

They asked me if I wanted to see photos of my parents' bodies. At first I said no, because I didn't want to remember my folks that way. Hendle went in and out of the room, as if more evidence was coming in all the time. I could see people looking into the room through the partially open door.

"Gary, the state's attorney is in the hall. He's talking the death sentence," she said. "We don't need a confession. We've got all the evidence we need. Your body wouldn't lie. The Galvanic Skin Response showed you weren't telling the truth in the test."

"Some of your answers were so bad they jumped right off the graph," Lowery added. "She's right. We don't need a confession. We have all the evidence we need."

They asked me if I had any weapons. I told them about a knife I vaguely remembered carrying. I don't usually carry knives because I always lose them. But I knew I put a knife in my pocket when I went home from work that week, because I needed it for transplanting and wanted to be able to find it first thing the next morning.

"What did you mean earlier, when you said you could help me?" I finally asked Lowery, when I was too exhausted to keep talking.

"All you're thinking about now is saving your own ass!" he screamed at me. "How can you be like that?"

I didn't know what to say and decided that maybe if I looked at the photos, something would jog my memory. But instead of just showing me the photos when I asked, Lowery started walking around the room, getting all worked up.

"You took a knife!" he screamed. "How could you? How could you do it? They trusted you. How could you kill your mother? How could you kill the woman who gave birth to you? How could you do THIS?"

With that, he slapped two very graphic pictures of my mom and dad down in front of me, like a winning hand in a poker game. I had never seen anything so awful. I winced and looked away. I think he expected some sort of emotional outburst and a confession. "I couldn't have killed my parents. I wouldn't have killed my parents," I pleaded, exhausted. "Let me go to sleep. We can continue this in the morning."

"No, Gary. You can't go to sleep. We've gone too deep. You'll just put up your barriers. We can't stop now," Lowery said.

SATURDAY MORNING, TWO THIRTY. They asked for more details about the knife. I had a dim memory of looking at a knife and putting it in my pocket. Later I realized the reason my memory was so dim was that it had been *Tuesday* night when I brought the knife home. I got up Wednesday at six to go to work and checked to make sure I didn't leave it at the house. It was still dark and I was half asleep. I didn't have the knife Thursday. I left it at the greenhouse Wednesday night.

"You don't have to remember, Gary," they told me. "We have the evidence. Something must have snapped. You know you can't keep this inside. You have to let it out. We all live on the edge, Gary. It could have happened to anyone. We don't need a confession. You were someone your parents knew and trusted. There was no robbery. Your mother's body was covered with blankets and pillows, like someone cared."

Lowery said they'd need blood samples from me; they had collected blood and tissue at the house that didn't belong to either of my parents. I just nodded.

I knew they had searched the greenhouse without permission when Lowery asked me about a knife they had found there. I never signed a consent form for them to search the greenhouse, which had a different address from my parents' house. I kept a little pot in a jar in my greenhouse, and at the time I had been worried about that enough to check the address on the search form.

"There was a dead cat in a box behind the greenhouse," Lowery said. "You were going to cut off its head in a satanic ritual, weren't you?" I explained it was a cat that belonged to a friend of mine. It was dying of feline leukemia and Al didn't want to pay the vet to put it to sleep or kill it himself, so he brought it over for me to shoot. I wasn't crazy about doing it, either, but Al was a good friend and the cat was very sick. I shot it and put it in the weeds along the fence, and planned to bury it once the ground thawed.

He ignored me. "Just tell us why you killed your parents," Lowery kept repeating. "There was no struggle. There was no robbery. Your body couldn't lie! You'll see, when you get a copy of the test in a couple of days. There were bloody fingerprints, Gary. The murderer had to be someone your parents trusted. We have the knife!"

I wanted to help. If I had killed my parents, I wanted to know about it. I tried to imagine doing it, or *how* I would do it. I agreed to create a hypothetical scenario of what I might have done if I *had* killed my mom and dad. Maybe that would help them put the pieces together of what *really* happened.

I summoned up an image of looking at the knife Wednesday morning.

"I looked at the knife," I started. I had a memory of seeing my mother two weeks before, as she worked out by the rug shop. But that day had been clear and sunny. The day she died, it was wet and windy.

"I would have gone into the living room. Then I would have gone out to the trailer, gone inside, seen my mother. My mother trusts me. I would have grabbed her by the hair."

I could see by the photos that someone had grabbed her by the hair and pulled it back. She didn't wear her hair that way. "And then I would have cut her throat," I managed to say, before the reality of the whole situation hit me. I started crying. It was the first time I cried since I found my father. "I would have caught her and laid her down, because I wouldn't want her to get hurt when she fell."

I said that because the photograph showed she had fallen backward and was lying in the middle of the trailer. Much later, I learned that was not even how she had fallen.

I collected myself and added, "And then I would have gone into the garage and killed my father. But this is just hypothetical. I have absolutely no memory of doing any of this."

They both said "okay" as they furiously wrote in their notes.

I remembered waking up at five. I remembered waking at seven, and again at eight and eight thirty. I remembered looking at the clock at eight forty-five and again at nine. The memory of that was very clear. I asked Hendle if it would have been possible for me to kill them in a complete blackout, then go back to bed and not remember any of it.

"Oh, yes!" she said very matter-of-factly, like it happened every day. "Yes, yes, you could have a blackout like that."

Up until this point, Lowery had been more of the accuser and Hendle had been a little more sympathetic. Now she looked at me and said, "Gary, you did it."

I just fell apart. I started to cry again. Sobbing, I put my head down on my arms. "I couldn't have done it," I cried. "Then there must be blood all over my clothes, all over the knife. I don't even remember putting on my shoes. There must be blood and mud all over my sheets." She just nodded.

That would explain all the evidence they had and why I was arrested right away. It would also explain why they talked about getting mental help at Elgin Hospital, and why I failed the lie test. Every time I would try to deny doing it, either Hendle or Lowery would say, "Gary, we have all the evidence we need. We know you did it."

By now, they were on either side of me. Lowery was very soft-spoken now, repeating those words over and over. "There was no struggle. It was someone they trusted. We know you did it. You did it, Gary. We have the knife. Your body wouldn't lie. You don't need to remember. We just need to know why."

I told them again and again that if I did it, I didn't remember. I was crying, confused. I would put my head down, raise it up to say something, and one of them would interrupt.

"There. You told the truth. We can see the real Gary come out! There! You did it again. We can see it in your eyes!"

Lowery was right next to me. I thought it was really insane that they had a murderer within two feet of a detective with a gun. It would be so easy for me to grab it. "I could just grab your gun and kill myself," I said, sobbing. "I want my sister and brother to hate me. I want them to see the pictures of my mother so they hate me as much as I hate myself." Hendle put her hand on my arm as I cried. How could she be so nice to me? I felt like the worst murderer in the world. I didn't see how anyone could possibly be kind to me.

Hendle suggested several reasons why I would kill my mom and dad. None of them made any sense. We talked about the theory of how people sabotage their own success. I had already told them how well things were going that spring, and how happy I had been. Finally, Hendle decided I was just tired of hurting my parents, of being a disappointment to them.

Sure, I was ashamed of getting divorced, but that hurt me more than anyone else and I was over it. My parents were very supportive of what I was doing. My dad often talked about how nice it would be if I could make the land a working farm again. He was glad I was working on motorcycles. We never argued. My dad's health was failing—he needed help in the shop and on the farm, and I was glad to do it. They had both told my sister how glad they were I had come back from Texas to live with them.

This went on for at least two more hours. They wouldn't let me deny anything, but there was nothing else I could say. We were all so tired. I put my head down on the table and asked again if we could stop and take it up later.

"No! We've come too far," Lowery said. "We have to keep going. You can't stop now. You'd just put up your defenses again and we'd have to break them back down."

SATURDAY MORNING, FIVE O'CLOCK. Pandre came in with an armful of clothing. "We'll take your clothes now, Gary," he said. If a policeman says he wants your clothes, and you're in the police station, and they are accusing you of killing your parents, you do what he says. When I started unbuttoning my shirt, Hendle turned around, seeming uncomfortable, and left. They took my wallet, my underwear, everything, even my shoes. They gave me a white prison shirt with the words "McHenry County Jail" written across the back, black pants, and jail slippers.

Lowery was hard with the questions again, getting excited and speaking loudly in an abusive way. We were both exhausted and I didn't have the energy to talk to him anymore, so I told Pandre I would talk with him instead. And when he said, "I just want to know the truth," I saw a ray of hope. Maybe he would listen. I started to tell him again what I really *did* know. About my parents, farming, my kids, my divorce, all the things Hendle and Lowery had been so eager to hear about last night.

Soon Pandre got impatient and snapped, "I just want to hear about Thursday morning!"

I began my story again. How I shut off the alarm at five, slept until seven, turned on the television to try to hear the weather. How I turned it off again in about twenty minutes, woke up, looked at the clock at eight and dozed off again.

Now Pandre lost control. He jumped up and yelled, "We don't want to hear about that! We just want to hear about you killing your parents!"

They weren't going to let me leave. They weren't going to let me sleep. They didn't care what I remembered. They had all the evidence against me. It was more than enough. I couldn't fight it any longer. I couldn't stand any more yelling. Maybe I had blacked out and killed them, after all. I just wanted this all to end.

SATURDAY MORNING, SEVEN O'CLOCK. I tried to piece together what could have happened the way the detectives described it. "I got up. I checked the knife in my pocket, saw my mother in the trailer and went up behind her—she trusted me," I said. "I cut her throat, caught her because I didn't want her to get hurt, and covered her with blankets because I cared. Then I went to the garage. My dad was walking away from me. He didn't hear me because he's hard of hearing. I cut his throat and let him fall."

"But I'm not going to sign a confession," I said, crying. "I have no memory of any of this. Everything I told you was something you told me, except for catching my mother. That's the way she looked in the photo." They asked me what I did next. I had no idea, because they hadn't told me that part yet. So I said I must have gone to work. They weren't at all upset when I said I wasn't going to sign a confession. After all, they said they already had all the evidence against me.

SATURDAY MORNING, TEN O'CLOCK. People were walking in and out after that. Someone brought in donuts. I remember starting to say to Hendle, "I killed my parents …" but then thought that if any of these people heard me say that and didn't know everything that happened before, they might think it's a confession. So I asked for a lawyer to tell him what had happened, the whole night, before I really *did* give a false confession.

"That's it, end of interview," they said, putting everything away in their folders. They didn't offer to bring an attorney in, and didn't ask if I wanted to call one. I figured I must have done something to make them angry.

About a half hour later they handed me over to another officer. They took mug shots, finger- and arm-printed me and stripped me out of the black and white jail trusty outfit. They made me take a shower, then put me in the standard prison garb, orange pants and an orange shirt. I spent a couple of hours alone in a jail cell until they brought me out to present me with a sheet of formal charges.

Two counts of first-degree murder.

Easter Weekend

A PAIR OF OFFICERS ARRIVED to lead me from the cell to the booking desk downstairs. As we reached the steps, I realized how easy it would be to dive headfirst over the handrail. With any luck, I would break my neck in the story-and-a-half fall. I still don't know what prevented me from taking the plunge at that moment.

Nothing about my body or mind seemed to belong to me. I still believed what Hendle, Lowery, and Pandre had told me repeatedly since three in the morning. I had killed my parents in a blackout. It seemed impossible, but they had the evidence. They wouldn't lie. They *couldn't* lie.

The booking officer didn't want me to go into any details about my case or situation. Her job wasn't to evaluate my mental or legal condition, just to get the information she needed to process me into the county jail. We went through her list of questions, and I answered "yes" when she asked me if I was suicidal. I wanted to die.

They put me in a holding cell, a concrete box with big glass windows directly across from the sergeant's desk so he could watch everything I did. Other prisoners came and went past the desk and my cell, which were about fifteen feet apart.

I lay on my cot, shivering. Complete turmoil does not even begin to describe my state of mind in those first hours. When I see film footage of birds caught in an oil slick, I think: "That's how it was." But even that seems inadequate.

I spent an hour and a half trying to comprehend what had happened to my parents—and what was happening to me now—but I knew I never would. So I hunkered down under the pillow so no one could see what I was doing, and chewed on toilet paper until it formed little balls. Then I inhaled and tried to suck the paper into my lungs.

When I went into convulsions from gagging, the guards noticed my thrashing and rushed into the cell. They made me cough the pieces out and I realized I was going to have to live after all.

I must have slept at some point, but I know I didn't eat anything that weekend. I wasn't hungry, even though I had had no real food since a few bites of the steak sandwich the police brought in on Friday evening.

On Sunday, I got a call from Ginger. We cried together on the phone and she said she found a lawyer for me. All I could tell her was that the police told me I had killed our parents. I can't imagine what was going through her mind. Did he really murder them in a blackout? Did her twin brother snap? If he didn't kill them, who did?

The fact that this was all happening on Easter weekend did not escape me. I still have trouble with the symbolism. In retrospect, though, my conversation with Ginger marked the beginning of my very long path to getting better, of coming back to myself. I tried to write everything I could remember about the past few days to give to the lawyer. I had a very short pencil and some brown paper towels, and I wrote around and around on the edge of the paper, drawing a little box in the middle that said "over." I doubt if any of it made any sense.

When I finally saw Ginger in person, she asked me some questions about what had happened over the past several days. Something I said made her realize I couldn't have killed our parents. From that point on, she became my strongest advocate.

After I started thinking about my situation and what really happened on Friday and Saturday, I figured I'd be free within two weeks of my arrest; the prosecutor would realize the nature of the interrogation, see that there was no evidence to back anything up, and let me go. I didn't think the police would lie, or that they were even *allowed* to lie.

I met the lawyer, Mark Gummerson, the next day. He believed me. But he was also the first person to tell me the police can and *do* lie. I didn't believe it until late June, when discovery was released and I read what the detectives said about the interrogation. Gummerson also told me innocent people do get convicted, but again, I naively thought the system would correct itself. My lawyer also said it would be impossible for me to sue the sheriff's department for what they did to me. Again, I didn't believe it. All these years later, I'm starting to see his point.

Public Opinion

THE APRIL 10 HEADLINE in the *Northwest Herald*, McHenry County's daily newspaper, read, "Richmond couple slain: Bodies found in workshop, farm trailer." Reporter Cyndi Naber's first story didn't mention that I had been taken to Woodstock for questioning.

RICHMOND—Police searched Friday for the killer or killers of an elderly Richmond couple.

Gary Gauger found the body of his father, Morris Gauger, on a workshop floor at the Gaugers' rural Richmond farm late Friday morning, McHenry County Undersheriff William T. Mullen said.

Gary, the only one of three children still living at home, called police at about 11:25 A.M. He said his father was dead and his mother, Ruth, was missing. Police found Mrs. Gauger's body in a trailer at the farm on Route 173. The 70-year-old woman sold rugs from the trailer, Mullen said. Mr. Gauger, 74, was a well-known antique motorcycle enthusiast, a mechanic and an excellent source for difficult-to-find parts.

Mullen said he did not know exactly when the couple died, although it appeared to have been "recent." He refused to say how they died.

"I'm not going to comment on the method," Mullen said. "They met a violent death, apparently homicide."

It was evident Friday afternoon that police were involved in an intense investigation. Marked and unmarked police cars lined the lengthy dirt driveway leading to the couple's farmhouse, barn, trailer and sheds.

By 1:30 P.M., at least nine detectives were combing the area. Some walked through a meadow west of the farm. Others fanned out to talk with neighbors. Mullen and Sheriff George H. Hendle were present, as was Deputy Coroner Judy Huemann.

By 4 P.M., State's Attorney Gary W. Pack, McHenry County Coroner Marlene A. Lantz, Deputy Coroner Mary Jo Coonen and Assistant State's Attorney Terry Nader had arrived.

Police would not allow reporters past the driveway entrance.

Several signs in the area direct motorists to the farm for Indian and sheepskin rugs. A few people stopped by Friday afternoon to inquire about rugs, but were turned away.

Others stopped by seeking the man they affectionately called Morrie. They, too, were disappointed. Police would tell most only that a "serious incident" had occurred. Others were interviewed. Consequently, some left wearing expressions of concern, while others left with worst fears confirmed.

Mullen said there was no apparent motive for the killings. Nothing appeared to be stolen.

Gary Gauger provided a statement to police. But he apparently had no clinching leads to offer.

"Gary was here last night and he was here this morning," Mullen said. "He heard nothing."

Besides Gary, the Gaugers are survived by another son, Gregg of Wisconsin, and a daughter, Ginger of Woodstock.

Anyone with any information is asked to call the McHenry County Sheriff's Department at 338-2145, Mullen said.

Naber wrote that police continued to "investigate their deaths" Friday night. Nothing was mentioned about interrogating their son for eighteen hours.

> April 11, 1993
> Son held in Richmond slayings
> By James Kimberly
> *The Northwest Herald*

RICHMOND—A Richmond man has been charged with stabbing his elderly parents to death less than 24 hours after he reported the crime.

Gary Gauger, 41, is being held in the McHenry County Jail in lieu of $10 million bond. He was charged Saturday morning with two counts of first-degree murder, said McHenry County Undersheriff William Mullen.

"We did not have him in custody (Friday night)—we were talking to him," Mullen said. "He made some statements that incriminated himself."

Gauger had called sheriff's police at about 11:25 A.M. Friday and told them he found his father, Morris Gauger, 74, dead. He said his mother, Ruth, 70, was missing. Sheriff's police found her in a trailer behind the house where the three of them lived.

Mullen released few details about the killings. Police believe they have the murder weapon but Mullen would not specify how many times the couple were stabbed, when the crime took place or what kind of knife or other object was used.

McHenry County State's Attorney Gary Pack said Saturday he has yet to decide whether he will seek the death penalty.

Gauger's friends and neighbors said police have charged the wrong man with the crime.

"If they found conclusive evidence that Gary did it, I would be shocked," said Fred Richter. "Part of the reason he doesn't work is he loves his parents so much. This was Nirvana—him and his parents working the farm."

Richter has rented a home from the Gaugers for five years. He believes they were victims of a robbery gone bad. Morrie Gauger's motorcycle repair shop had a reputation for finding rare parts and Ruth Gauger sold Native American rugs from the trailer where her body was found.

"It's impossible that Gary did it (and) being as pleasant as Ruth and Morrie are, I can't imagine anyone having a grudge against them," Richter said.

Gary Gauger is unemployed. During the summers, he sold vegetables from a roadside stand.

"He's the kind of guy who gets silly when he drinks, he does not get angry," Richter said.

Others who knew the family agreed with Richter.

"I've known him all my life and I've never seen any violent streaks," said friend Ed Mitchell. "They were always good to him, I've never seen them argue."

Charles and Ann Marik have lived across the street from the Gaugers for 12 years. They were shocked by the slayings.

"You move to rural America, you think something like this would never happen across the street," Ann Marik said.

Amy R. Mack of the *Northwest Herald* quoted "inside sources" as saying my parents' murder "*was a crime of passion, a very violent crime*" and that the killer used a large buck knife to "*slice through almost to the spine*" before fracturing their skulls.

Of course, the inside sources were the police themselves, even though at first they refused to confirm what they had leaked to the press in the first place.

In the April 12 issue, Mullen was still saying that I made incriminating statements about myself. *"If we thought we still have a murderer on the loose, if we weren't so sure of our offender, we would have alerted the community to take extra precautions."*

Police look into 'lost' day after murder, said the headline over Jill Janov's story in the April 13 *Northwest Herald.*

WOODSTOCK — Police want to know why accused murderer Gary Gauger waited more than a day before reporting his father's death and his mother's disappearance.

Investigators say Gauger, 41, Route 173, admitted Saturday that he killed his elderly parents Thursday morning.

But little is known about what happened between Wednesday, when the couple was last seen, and Friday morning, when Gauger called police.

"We still have to do some background work," McHenry County Sheriff George Hendle said. "We've got to talk to neighbors. We're going to have to try and fill in a period of time."

Neighbors saw the couple for the last time Wednesday. The couple was seen outside their home-based motorcycle and rug shops on Route 173, where they lived with their son, one of three children.

Gauger called police just before noon Friday after he and a customer found Morrie Gauger's body in his workshop behind the house. Gauger initially reported that his father, a 74-year-old dealer of antique motorcycle parts, was dead and his mother was missing.

Investigators found the bludgeoned body of Ruth Gauger, 70, in a trailer where she sold rugs.

Sources say Gauger allegedly slit his parents' throats with a buck knife, nearly slicing off their heads, and then fractured their skulls.

Gauger initially told police he last saw his parents eating dinner Wednesday night. But after hours of questioning, sources said, Gauger implicated himself and even identified the murder weapon.

"He admitted doing it," Hendle said. "He was aware of circumstances that only the offender would know."

Hendle said police took several knives from buildings on the farm. The knives and clothing will be sent to a crime lab for testing.

Charged with two counts of first-degree murder, Gauger is being held on $10 million bond in the McHenry County Jail. He appeared in court Monday with his lawyer, Mark Gummerson. Gummerson said he planned to interview Gauger Monday night.

Gummerson asked police to preserve the tape recording of Gauger's 911 call for help. He also wants detectives to save their handwritten notes taken during their investigation.

Gummerson said he made the request because police typically shred their notes after typing formal reports. Gummerson said he also will ask to inspect the crime scene.

If convicted, Gauger faces between 20 years in prison and the death penalty.

McHenry County State's Attorney Gary Pack said Gauger could be sentenced to death only if he is convicted of both murders.

But Pack said he needs more information regarding motive before deciding whether to seek the death penalty.

––––––––

PEOPLE WHO WERE NOT CLOSELY FAMILIAR with my case got all their information from the newspaper. Couple slain. Son confesses. Until just before the trial, that was the only information released, so of course, that's what people believed. Our attorney told everyone in my family not to talk to the press, so the police basically had the *Northwest Herald* all to themselves.

I called my childhood friends Lars and Sue Anderson that first week and asked them not to believe what they read in the papers. "I didn't kill my parents," I told them. Lars said he had heard about the murders from a woman he worked with at Anderson's Candy in Richmond. He called Sue at the veterinary clinic where she worked, and she asked him where I was. He told her that I had been arrested, but that was all they knew until Lars talked to Ginger after she and Evan arrived from New Mexico. They were two of my closest friends and their only source of information was the newspaper.

I didn't request permission to go to my parents' memorial service, which was held at a local restaurant a month after the murders. If they had even allowed me to go, I would have been put in shackles, accompanied by two police officers at my expense.

But that wasn't the reason I didn't go. The thought that all my parents' friends thought I was a killer was just too much. I grew up with those people. They were customers of the motorcycle shop and I considered them my friends, too. There was no way I could show up at that service and have everybody think I killed my parents.

Ginger knew I didn't kill them, and had the added burden of knowing that the real killer was still out there. She installed two-by-fours across the doors and got a dog for protection. Evan carried a .32 caliber pistol on his belt.

Waiting for Justice

For the first month, I alternated between incapacitating depression and the belief that the police had all the evidence in the world—but that my sister and lawyer weren't telling me about it because they were afraid I'd try to kill myself again. It took me about a month and a half to shake that thought.

After a couple of days in observation, they put me in the medical pod. There were some interesting guys in there. They were all on meds and had to be closely supervised. Mark Gummerson had told me not to talk to anyone from the county, but I did have an interview with the county psychologist and told him and his aide that the police were framing me. I also talked to the chaplain and told him the same thing. I'm sure none of them believed me at the time, but I bet they remember those conversations to this day.

I liked Gummerson, but he wanted $50,000 up front and we didn't have it. He told Ginger the trial could run as high as $200,000. We didn't have that kind of money. Once I realized the cops had lied to me and about me, I tried to convince Ginger to let me have a court-appointed attorney—I figured the worst public defender in the world could get me off. But Ginger sensed that I was in more trouble than I did, and hired two new lawyers to handle my case.

William Davies and Russell Miller took over my case on April 21. I was unimpressed with Davies from the start. He wouldn't talk to me about the case. He just didn't seem interested. I liked Miller better, but he never seemed prepared for anything. He always looked like he had slept in his clothes. And yet we paid them $25,000 up front and $200 per hour *each*.

I was in the medical pod with about six other men. One of them, Raymond Wagner, was a hyperactive guy in his early twenties. He was the unhappiest person I had ever met in my life. He apparently was in the pod because he had tried to put his fist through a plate glass window and ended up with a broken hand. I was there because of the toilet paper incident.

The pod consisted of six or seven cells, two common rooms, and in the center, a glass-enclosed nurses' station with access to the guard tower. On the other side, again in a glass-enclosed room, lived the treeclimbers. "Treeclimbers" was the name for the psychiatric observation unit and its inhabitants. People like me were sent there after medical observation unless the authorities were sure there was a strictly physical problem. There was one dayroom, and everybody sat there all day, playing poker and watching TV. I had no choice but to talk to Ray Wagner for weeks.

Months later, at the trial, I realized that Wagner, who had previous felony convictions for theft and burglary, had seen me as his ticket to a reduced sentence. He added his own twist to the lies already being told about me, and his testimony as a "jailhouse snitch" would contribute to my conviction.

The only true part of Wagner's later testimony was that I danced with a broom and sang antiwar songs. I think I sang *White Boots Marching in a Yellow Land*—Phil Ochs, one of my favorites. Taken out of context, I appeared unstable. But I was just trying to get Ray to crack a smile. I had never seen a gloomier guy.

My main goal in the psych ward was to keep my sanity. I had a cellmate during my stay there, one of the few times I had one during my months in McHenry County. I still don't know why they put me in with Bernie. If I was the vicious killer they said I was, they were placing him in a very dangerous situation. Bernie was about eighteen, but had the mind of a twelve-year-old. He apparently had some kind of sexual encounter with an underage kid, which landed him in jail. It wasn't surprising that he lived a troubled life. He had a sugar imbalance and a lot of mental problems.

Ginger, Evan, and Gregg came to see me every few days. I don't even like to think about how hard it was for them, especially Ginger. When she finally was allowed to go back into the house, she said it felt like space aliens had abducted everyone. We were all just *gone*.

I was in treeclimbers half of April, all of May, and the first week of June. I never had a formal psychiatric exam. They just kept an eye on me and eventually decided I was able to move into general population.

———————

THE MCHENRY COUNTY JAIL was in a brand-new building and they had thought everything out. It was cold in the building twenty-four hours a day, seven days a week, 365 days a year. The thin orange prison suits provided no warmth at all.

It was all temperature and climate controlled. We had the choice of sitting on a steel bench or the concrete floor during the day. It was warmer in the cells, but it was an all-or-nothing proposition. Stay in your cell all day and just get out to get your meals, or leave your cell and sit in the freezing common area. It was so boring in the cell that almost everybody wanted to get out.

They controlled our diet very closely. They gave us absolutely the minimum calorie count they could and still keep us somewhat healthy. We lost weight. We were starving. We were freezing.

Again, this was all thought out. Most of the people in the jail were kids. If you got picked up for a serious crime, it would take between four and six months for your case to come to trial. The prosecutors wanted some of these guys to cop a guilty plea to get them out of there. If you're sitting in jail for three months freezing and starving, you're more likely to do that.

Our daily routine started at five thirty in the morning, when the guards would wake us up for breakfast. We'd take our showers in the bathroom off the common area, then go to the table in the main room where they would feed us. Food trading was not allowed, but I would always take a chance and trade everything I could for coffee—my only pleasure. When I got caught, they put me in lock-down for the infraction.

After breakfast, you'd go back to your cell for a head count before going out to the main room again. They didn't let us keep our towels after our showers, because we would have used them as pillows to cushion the hard, cold benches. We could have generated some body heat using the weight machines, but most of us didn't have enough energy.

We were also allowed to use the gym three times a week for an hour. It was only half a gymnasium with a basketball hoop, but it also had a big, louvered window up at the top, and that was the only time we could smell fresh air. The guards would stand outside the window and smoke cigarettes, so every now and then we got a whiff of tobacco.

Other than that, our only other activities were church services and Bible study with Community Uplifting People. We formed our own Bible study group in our pod. These sessions were nice, because we actually got to interact with somebody from the outside. There was also a library we could visit once a week. We didn't have any chores or responsibilities beyond keeping ourselves clean and not stinking so bad that the other prisoners would complain.

The vast majority of the prisoners were seventeen- to twenty-five-year-old McHenry County kids who acted like twelve-year-olds. They were in for things like busting up a cop car when they got picked up for doing drugs or drinking. Repeat DUIs. Stealing. Most of them were in what we called the Thunderdome pod, which was a little wilder than the rest. It consisted of six or seven pods together, including psych.

Two guys who had held up a Church's Chicken in Woodstock a couple of months after the Brown's Chicken massacre in Palatine, Illinois, were in there. One was an all-American football player type, a nice guy from the Midwest. He and another guy decided to go into Church's Chicken at closing time with a gun to rob the place. He's lucky he's still not in jail. I saw him in the local Farm and Fleet store about six months after he got out, and it was really good to see him. He had been in my Bible study group and was really a good guy—just another kid who had been drinking and screwed up.

There were so many stories. I met another nice guy with a drinking problem who said he was trying to wash his car one day when a kid kept bugging him. Finally, the man pushed the kid away. The kid went home crying to his mom, and later, when the man got home, the police were waiting for him at his door. They arrested him for DUI and aggravated battery. He was a fairly regular guy, and we got to be pretty good friends. After about a month and a half, he pleaded guilty to a felony rather than sit in jail. He ran off to New Mexico and within a very short time the game wardens there arrested him for violating his parole and eating prickly pear cactus, a protected species. Apparently he was roasting the prickly pears to get the thorns off. Three months later, while I was in the same pod, he was sent back to Woodstock with a huge blister on his hand—when the wardens approached him in New Mexico, he had put his hand down on a prickly pear by mistake and the thorns hadn't come out yet. So now he was back with a parole violation on a felony charge. He could have sat it out for six months and fought the original charge down to a misdemeanor—which is all it was in the first place.

———

THE GRAND JURY CHARGED ME in May. Two counts of murder made me eligible for the death penalty in Illinois.

A story in the May 6, 1993, *Northwest Herald* said:

> WOODSTOCK—A grand jury Wednesday charged Gary Gauger with the murders of his parents, making him eligible for the death penalty.
> . . . Before filing murder charges, grand jurors heard testimony that Gauger confessed to stabbing Morris "Morrie" Gauger, 74, and his wife Ruth, 70.
> McHenry County Sheriff's police said Gauger told them details only the murderer would know.
> Police did not reveal those details, but said Gauger identified the murder weapon—a buck knife that police recovered. . .

I wasn't at the grand jury proceedings; that's the prosecutor's show. I pleaded not guilty to the charges. The judge gave the prosecutor until May 25 to turn over all discovery, but they didn't even start giving us the information until mid-June. It wasn't until I read through discovery a few times that I realized something was missing. I realized the police were taking the two hypothetical statements and mixing them together. According to their reports, the events of the interrogation between one and five A.M. never happened. They said I was just chatting with them until five. I wasn't under arrest, even though I was sitting there in a jail outfit. Then I suddenly became very still and uttered statements only the killer would know.

I don't think the detectives realized what a good job they were doing, brainwashing a susceptible person in extreme shock. They just made up their minds I was guilty and decided to get a confession. They knew how to do it and did it. Beverly Hendle had taken a course on interrogation techniques just weeks prior to my arrest.

In July I practically begged Ginger to drop Davies and Miller and let me use a public defender. By now I knew the detectives were lying and was sure that it would be an easy case to win. I thought we could go with a public defender and have him work with a paid lawyer to make sure he was doing the job. But I found out you can't do that. You can either afford to hire a lawyer or you can't.

Ginger had heard horror stories about public defenders and didn't want to go that route. She begged me not to drop Davies. And she was probably right—public defenders don't really fight your case; they just make the system run more smoothly.

And yet Davies, the well-paid lead lawyer on the case, seldom came to see me the summer before I went to trial. He came to the jail a few times to ask a quick question, then left. Lawyers could arrange for a conference room, but he preferred to talk on a phone through a glass wall rather than go to the trouble. And he never had me work on the case at all.

Gummerson had warned me that this kind of lawyer would take a lower retainer then pump up expenses. He said the legal costs wouldn't be any lower in the long run. I could see Davies doing it—the only consolation was that I knew he was doing it. And in fact, the bill from Davies and Miller came in at about $210,000. Certainly no bargain over Gummerson.

Later, when the case finally went to trial, Davies and Miller were working ten hours a day at $200 an hour and weren't making any progress. During the two or three days of jury selection, I remember thinking, *Pick this guy. Pick that guy. C'mon . . . the dumbest guy out there will find me not guilty. This is costing me four dollars a minute!*

My lawyers' attitude was similar to one you might find around a hospital. I'm the doctor and you're just the nurse, so you don't know anything at all. Davies didn't care about my input, even though it was my life on the line and my parents who had been murdered.

"I'll do the lawyering, you grow tomatoes," he told me.

Cowlin's Court

YOU'VE SEEN IT dozens of times on TV: The courtroom is silent as a side door opens and the defendant enters the courtroom, stony-faced and serious, dressed in conservative clothes for the benefit of the judge and jury. I don't remember now how I felt when I walked through that door myself for the first time. Maybe I was just happy to get the trial under way, to receive the acquittal I was sure I would get, and go home. I figured it would be a slam-dunk.

At any rate, I looked the part, wearing a blue sports jacket of Evan's, beige Dockers, a white shirt, and a red tie. Each morning, prison guards led me from my cell to a little staging area off the courtroom, where I would dress for my day on trial. At the end of each day's testimony, they took me back into the room, took off my trial clothes, gave me a strip search, and dressed me in my usual orange uniform before escorting me back to my cell.

Davies met me in this room about ten minutes before the trial started each day. There was little conversation between us, and even less lawyer-client advice. We came out together take our places at the table. He took an aisle seat to my right so he could jump up easily if he needed to object to something, and Miller sat next to me on the left.

I could see my friends and family already seated in the gallery. Ginger, Evan, Gregg, Sue, and Lars were there every day, but I wasn't allowed to say anything to them. I wasn't in any kind of restraints, but a cop sat right behind me all during the trial. You could tell he was ready to make a move if I even shifted slightly in my chair.

Red-faced and puffy, Judge Henry L. Cowlin melted into his robe. And he was often distracted. Anytime something was going on—even when the prosecutor was talking—he was doing something else, talking to his clerk, or sitting with his eyes closed. This became even more extreme the day I testified.

Then they led the jury in. There was a man with Ted Koppel-style hair. A man who looked like an insurance salesman. A young woman in overalls, and another perky young woman who was a grocery clerk. Most of the time when I looked over at them, they would smile at me. The day I testified, though, they quit smiling. I still don't know what it all meant. Maybe someone told them not to look sympathetic when the defendant took the stand. But even when I didn't get smiles, I really wasn't worried. They just needed to hear all the facts.

There was no physical evidence, there were no witnesses, no murder weapon, no motive, nothing that would make anyone believe I was guilty. Even Philip Prossnitz, McHenry County's assistant state's attorney, said he had little physical proof to tie me to the crimes, and would instead base his case on circumstantial evidence and my so-called "confession." I was confident. There was just no chance a jury would convict.

Of course, I was very wrong.

The signs of what was to come should have been apparent to me even from the testimony in the pretrial proceedings. There was a two-day hearing on whether to ban the confession, our argument being they had no reason to detain me in the first place and that the confession was forced. Cowlin had ruled against me, saying my behavior alone was unusual enough to make the cops suspicious.

PROSSNITZ: *When the body of his mother is discovered, there is no emotion. Why is there no emotion? The police came to the conclusion that he knew the body would be found there. Why had he taken those steps to go into the garage? Because the police came to the logical conclusion the body was in there. Why does he, when he gets into the garage, not go to the body, but goes in this ridiculous route looking for a part? Because he knows the body was there. Why does he not try to force the small lock open on the trailer where his mother was? Because he knew her body was there. The absence of emotion and all of this taken together from the standpoint of the police, to have a defendant here—leads to proof beyond a reasonable doubt there is probable cause to detain him and question him.*

The same refrain echoed throughout the trial. *The issue wasn't concern or non-concern specifically, but his attitude and demeanor concerning the death of his parents seemed to be . . . I guess nonchalant would be the best way I can describe it,* Detective Lowery said. *Not a typical emotional reaction. And I didn't know the cause for him to act that way.*

My lawyer didn't press the issue on how a man can be guilty based on what a cop feels is an abnormal reaction to his parents' deaths—as if anyone can predict how someone else (or he himself) would act faced with a similar shock. He did, however, get Lowery to admit there was no physical evidence against me.

Photo by Julie Von Bergen

The McHenry County Courthouse in Woodstock, Illinois.

Lowery said I was a suspect before midnight, but *not* under arrest. *So was there any reason why, to continue this interrogation—which had lasted for approximately twelve hours—you couldn't stop and go on the next day and give him an opportunity to rest?* Miller asked.

LOWERY: *Well, he didn't show any signs of needing sleep and was alert and answering our questions. I felt it was important to continue talking as long as he would talk because at any time he could tell us he didn't want to talk anymore.*

MILLER: *You realized, Detective, based upon your experience as a policeman, that the more fatigued people become, the more susceptible they are to suggestion?*

LOWERY: *I don't know if I have had any experience in the powers of suggestion or not.*

MILLER: *Let me rephrase that. Have you heard of sleep deprivation?*

LOWERY: *Sure.*

MILLER: *And what do you know about or how would you characterize or define sleep deprivation?*

LOWERY: *Someone who is not allowed to sleep or does not sleep for long periods of time.*

MILLER: *At seven in the morning on April 10 it is your testimony that Mr. Gauger did not appear to be tired or fatigued at all?*

LOWERY: *Not at all.*

MILLER: *Did you ever tell him that you thought he was lying?*

LOWERY: *No. I specifically had said to him that I felt that his account of things did not make sense . . . at one point in time I indicated to him, when he said his parents were missing and he didn't check the hospitals, didn't check the motorcycle shop or the rug trailer, but he had checked everything else, I said, "The two places they might most likely be on the premises, other than the home. It just didn't make sense that you didn't check that."*

MILLER: *Isn't it true that prior to seven in the morning, when you indicated Gary gave information that he had killed his parents, you asked him to explain hypothetically how he would kill his parents?*

LOWERY: *I don't recall.*

He "didn't recall" Hendle or Pandre asking me about hypothetical scenarios, either. For a cop testifying at trial, the best way avoid perjuring yourself is to say you "don't recall."

LOWERY: *What he said prior to that with Beverly Hendle during that point in time when I wasn't part of the interview, I wasn't a witness to. When I came back in at ten, he made the statement, "I have killed my parents."... No, he didn't appear to be tired at fatigued at ten. After he made the "I have killed my parents" remark was the first time I saw him express emotion and he cried, especially in regard to his parents. He didn't appear fatigued at all.*

MILLER: *Did you ever, prior to him allegedly saying that he had killed his parents, suggest to him that he had killed his parents?*

Prossnitz objected that the question wasn't relevant.

MILLER: *Judge, again, the basis of the motion is mental, psychological coercion. At ten in the morning, up for twenty-five hours, he had been interviewed for approximately twenty-two hours by the officers. I suggest that any suggestions made by these officers are relevant to the state of mind of our client and goes directly to psychological and mental coercion.*

Miller continued, asking Lowery if the purpose of keeping me talking was that he hoped I would say something to incriminate myself.

LOWERY: *At any time I would talk to an individual, if they were a witness or part of a criminal act, I would hope they would say something that would either help resolve the crime or incriminate themselves. However, I felt if Mr. Gauger at any time would have said, "Hey, this interview is history," we would have been giving him a ride back home.*

Why the prison clothes? my lawyer asked. Was it to humiliate me? Couldn't someone have gone to the house to get a change of clothes?

LOWERY: *I don't want to say we didn't have someone available. I'm sure we probably could have. I suppose we took the handy way out.*

My lawyers said the way the detectives misrepresented the results of my polygraph test—telling me I didn't pass—led to the false "confession" the next morning. I was operating under a twisted reality, thinking I had failed the test although all that really happened was the results were inconclusive because of my fatigue. But of course the prosecution couldn't go along with that, since the detectives had to stick to their story that I never showed any signs of being tired.

Prossnitz dismissed the whole cause and effect argument. *I don't think because someone is up all night they are suddenly going to confess to a double homicide of their parents that they didn't commit, regardless of what someone told them*, he told the judge. In fact, convincing a vulnerable suspect that he committed a crime—regardless of the truth—is a typical interrogation ploy. But in this case, he was partially right. I never did confess.

Just before jury selection was to start, Prossnitz announced he had a new witness. He said Al Eastridge, a friend of my parents, had come forward just a week before to report that two months before they were killed, my mother told him that I had beat her. He also said I was so drunk at Christmas they had to tie me to the bed. He said he heard my voice in the background yelling, "Untie me . . . untie me! Come in here, untie me!"

I still don't know why he would make up a story like that, or what made him come forward at that moment. I suspect the police tricked him into concocting the story. They needed something spectacular at that point, since there was nothing to tie me to the crimes. They wanted to give the impression that I was a deranged, violent drunk, I guess. Although the judge ruled that Eastwood could testify, Prossnitz told the judge later he was having trouble reaching his last-minute witness. Eastridge never did take the stand.

But the damage had already been done. The story saying I beat my mother was big news in the *Northwest Herald*. Who knows if the people in the jury pool read it just as they were heading in to be interviewed? Several prospective jurors were excused because they said they already had opinions about the case from newspaper articles, but how many more were subconsciously influenced by them?

Prossnitz knew exactly what he was doing by introducing Eastridge when he did. And a couple of days later, as jury interviews continued, he announced that two inmates reported they had heard me confess. Jailhouse testimony like this is very suspect, considering the opportunities for a trade of "information" for a shorter sentence. In this case, the stories hadn't even been verified. But to someone who was leaning toward believing the police version of events, this kind of headline could tip the balance.

And so went the trial, one straight-faced lie after another from three law enforcement officers. I sat at the table with Miller and Davies, waiting for them to expose the lies in a direct way. If they did their job, I figured, surely the jury would see through this nonsense.

The police said I was not emotional enough, even though it was obvious from the 911 tape played in court that I was near tears and very upset, and even though Ed Zender and Traci Fozkos testified I was at a loss as to the whereabouts of my folks and that I was visibly distraught after we found my dad's body. Apparently there is a certain level of emotion that cops expect you to reach in order to be considered innocent until proven guilty.

The police said I was not under arrest when my mother's body was found, even though witnesses testified that police said, *Don't let him go! Put him in the car!* right after they found my mother's body. They patted me down and locked me in the back of a marked squad car with a caged partition . . . but, according to the police, it was just so they'd be able to find me quickly if they had any questions, not because I was a suspect. I was still free to leave, according to them, although the cop who had guarded me did testify that he kept me under constant watch.

Beverly Hendle echoed Lowery when she testified with a straight face, *I can't say exactly when Gary became a suspect. But until he confessed, he was free to leave all night.*

They said they ate dinner with me at about ten thirty that night because they wanted to "be polite."

I can imagine what the jury thought. She was under oath, so she must be telling the truth. That was the law. I wasn't under *interrogation* all night. I was just being interviewed. They didn't think I *did* anything, for heaven's sake. I was just helping out. Ironically, that's exactly what I thought I was doing, at first. I was just trying to think of anything I could that would help the investigation.

According to Hendle, I told her I smoked marijuana all day Thursday—morning, noon, and night. I told her I was half Betazoid. Lowery denied taking any notes until five thirty A.M. Saturday. Hendle believed Lowery took notes, but they never were produced in discovery. Hendle photocopied those notes, but didn't bother to read them, even though she was the lead detective.

Lowery claimed he didn't make notes, yet quickly danced around the issue of writing the words "Jesus Freak" in those very same notes. He said he wrote those words, "or something like that," but said they didn't refer to me. *I wanted to make sure I asked him about his religious background in regard to it because he had made some statements about this,* he told the court. *The reference was just to remind myself to ask him about his demeanor in things which came up when he discussed how he had been in a commune, how he had lived in*

Texas, and one of his children had been born on a bus in a commune. These kinds of things.

They said they never mentioned that I could get help if I cooperated. They never mentioned Elgin State Hospital. Never hinted in any way that I might be mentally ill.

No need for me to volunteer for a polygraph, since they didn't think of me as a suspect. As a matter of fact, *they* said they suggested it, not me. Frankenberry never told them why he couldn't pass me, and they never asked. Up until the polygraph exam, they said we talked mainly about myself and my life, with me directing the conversation and doing most of the talking.

Frankenberry testified that he informed me that my parents' throats had been cut. He acknowledged that this kind of shocking information can present an adverse effect on the results if the person is presented with it just prior to taking the test. But the real meat of the matter—that my test results were inconclusive because of my fatigue—was not allowed into testimony.

Hendle told the court that no one ever told me that the "skin test" showed I was lying. She testified that she didn't even know what the Galvanic Skin Response was. *I don't understand the mechanism of the polygraph with blood pressure, heartbeat, respiration, self-worth, so any technical information he gives me doesn't mean anything to me,* she said.

Lowery denied asking me how I would cut somebody's throat—hypothetically or otherwise—as I left the polygraph room. According to them, no officer ever asked me, "How could you kill the mother who gave birth to you?" Pandre said there were never any other officers in the interrogation room, even though a police report said there was. None of them ever told me they had a stack of evidence against me or that they didn't believe me. I never made a hypothetical confession, just a straightforward statement. They claimed I said the day of my parents' murders was the best I ever had.

They said I wasn't even under arrest when Pandre brought in the jail clothes for me. Yet even Hendle testified she left the examination room at five thirty (not after my "confession" as the others said) so I could change into them.

According to the cops my confession just fell into their laps. They did admit in court that between twelve thirty and five thirty A.M. I had *repeatedly* said, "If I killed my parents, I don't remember doing it." Yet they never tried to explain why I would say this if there hadn't been some hypothetical or "what-if" speculating going on, and also said I'd said nothing specific to implicate myself before seven thirty. Why would I ever say such a thing, if I wasn't reacting to a hypothetical situation I was asked to elaborate on?

Most troubling is why they never explained why they never even *tried* to get any kind of a record of my "confession," even at ten A.M. They said they didn't ask about weapons, nothing. Lowery just said he felt they were walking on eggs and was afraid I'd shut down the conversation if he pushed me. If he was so afraid I would shut down, why did he and Pandre leave the room at a crucial point and just leave Hendle to watch me? It made no sense. All those hours of interrogation, and they just walked away after I "confessed," not even bothering to record anything?

I had signed a consent form at eleven thirty Friday night to be recorded and videotaped . . . had "steered" the conversation all night long and into the morning, gave up my clothes willingly, suddenly blurted out my "confession" at seven thirty, talked for another three hours . . . and yet they were walking on eggshells, afraid I'd shut down the conversation.

Beverly Hendle said it would have been too much trouble to tape the whole interrogation—who would have wanted to take the time to go all through that again? When she said that, you'd think the jaws of everybody on the jury would have dropped to the floor.

According to Pandre, he told me at seven thirty Saturday morning that he just wanted the truth. My answer, according to him: *I woke up, got dressed and patted my pocket, checking for my knife. I saw my mother in the trailer, went out, came up behind her (she trusted me), cut her throat, and caught her because I didn't want her to get hurt. Then I covered her with pillow and blankets because I cared. I then went to the garage, and saw my father walking away from me. I went up behind him, which was easy because he was hard of hearing and couldn't hear me. I cut his throat and let him fall. Then I just went about my business.*

They testified that when they asked me about the weapon, I said, "Everything you need will be in the trailer and the shop." They said I made two cutting motions when I came up behind my father, and indicated I grabbed his hair. That's not in the original police report, but was new testimony at trial.

They made a big deal about me grabbing my mother's hair and about the fact that her hair had been pulled out. They said there was no way I could have known about that detail if I hadn't been there. But the photo they showed me in the middle of the night showed her hair was pulled back and out. I kept pointing that out to them that morning, but they had just looked at me blankly.

And at seven thirty A.M., in fact, that was all the police knew. The autopsies didn't begin until twelve thirty on Saturday afternoon. They showed that both my parents were repeatedly hit in the head before their throats were cut, and that their throats were not cut until after they had fallen. My mother had been hit so hard a plug of her skull had actually broken free of the rest of her skull. My father had also been stabbed in the side.

The police also lied about something that happened well after the murders. On April 19, my sister and brother-in-law were allowed into the house to get some papers, the first time they had gone in since my parents' deaths. Ginger found a large amount of money my parents had in the house (something the cops had completely missed during their search), and a police officer testified that he clearly remembered sitting on the floor counting it with

Evan, yet he couldn't remember even one word of the conversation Beverly Hendle was having with Ginger at the kitchen table just a few feet away. Even so, he was able to remember what they *didn't* talk about.

What Hendle told my sister that day was that hypothetical situations are used all the time to spur a confession. On the stand, though, Hendle said she never even sat at the table, and never had any conversation with Ginger.

Prossnitz tried to convince the jurors that I killed my parents so I could inherit the farm and motorcycle shop inventory. He pegged the value of the 200-acre farm at $1.4 million, and the inventory at more than $100,000.

His argument was that the murder weapon was one of the approximately two dozen knives the police confiscated, including five from my greenhouse. None of them had a single trace of any evidence that showed they were linked to the crimes. There was no sign of blood on any of them. They weren't hidden away or dumped somewhere to hide the evidence. In fact, the pathologist, Dr. Lawrence Blum, said while any of the knives *could* have been used to kill my parents, so could any number—an infinite number—of knives, not just the ones we owned.

I cannot point to a knife and say that was the knife, no sir, he testified. *Any sharp-edged object would be capable of causing those throat wounds.*

There was no evidence of me trying to hide anything. My dirty work clothes were analyzed, the contents of the drain traps were removed and tested, everything was searched . . . and nothing was ever found to link me to the crime. Never was my testimony discredited, beyond the obvious disagreements about the interrogation.

Ray Wagner, my fellow "treeclimber" and jailhouse snitch from my first days in the McHenry County Jail, did testify against me, saying that (after knowing me just one day) I admitted to him that I killed my parents after they caught me running a con.

Wagner was in jail on a 240-day sentence for driving on a revoked license. On April 19 or 20, he testified, he was in the medical pod with me. The next day, he said, the two of us were playing chess when I asked him to call me Gary Manson or Gary Bundy, because I had done something really bad. Then, Wagner said, he asked me if I was the guy from Richmond. I said yeah. When he asked me why I did it, I told him, "It seemed like the thing to do at the time." Then I flipped over the chess game, said I was through, and took off through the room shrieking, "Whoop . . . whoop! And singing some song."

Wagner testified he had told his story because it was the right thing to do. He told his attorney he had a "piece of fruit" to run by the judge and state's attorney, and he would tell everything about his conversation with Gary Manson in return for his own release from jail.

The first chance he had to get near me, he took it. We met after a church service, gave each other a hug, and I asked him how his mom was doing. She had been very sick and was also taking care of Wagner's child.

This is a typical jailhouse snitch technique, and sometimes, after the snitch gets close to the mark, the police even feed the snitch information only the killer would know. I don't know if this was the case with Wagner. His testimony was first brought to our attention June 24. It was full of holes and quickly exposed. But Ray Wagner received early release from jail because of his testimony. It's pathetic that the state even used a witness like that.

We presented our case in two days of the two-week trial, including my brother's, brother-in-law's, and sister's testimony and my own, which lasted five and a half hours. My lawyers didn't have anyone else who knew both me and my parents testify, which I felt was a big mistake. Anyone who knew me well would know I couldn't possibly do something like this. Maybe the reason the jury members stopped smiling at me that day had something to do with the leadership provided by Judge Cowlin. Several people in the courtroom noticed some odd behavior on his part, as did my own lawyers. They were left with the delicate job of confronting him.

Whether you know it or not, or realize it, or not, people in the audience have noticed that when Gary testifies, you make faces, Davies told the judge. *At one time, you rolled your eyes. You do things that imply to a jury if they happen to be watching you at that moment that Gary is not telling the truth.*

COWLIN: *Well, I may have been rubbing my eyes, but I'm rubbing my eyes because I'm having a little trouble with my eyes itching. I am not in any way . . . I listen to what he says. I'm not going to worry about which way it goes. I do lean back, as Mr. Prossnitz says. I have leaned back in my chair from time to time. Something is fogging my vision. What it is, whether it's something in the courthouse, or not, I don't know, but there is something that causes me to get a little foggier sometimes, and it is not my eyesight is bad or anything of that sort, but it is something else and I in no way have caused this. If this came out of one source that is in the courtroom, I would be more suspicious of it because of a recent incident that has occurred and I know the person who is involved or who did it is the person in my courtroom.*

No, Davies answered, at least eight to ten people mentioned his "faces."

I should maybe do like Judge Brody used to do, Cowlin continued. *He used to just turn, wheel around in his chair, turn his back to everything. There are times when you may get the thought that I may fall asleep but I have not fallen asleep at any time. I'm sitting there listening and I have my own way of concentrating.*

On May 10, the court had ordered the prosecution to turn over all evidence to us by May 24. Yet we received absolutely nothing until June 15. Hendle said she took notes in both shorthand and longhand during the "conversation" with me the night of the interrogation and said she turned over a photocopy of them to the state's attorney. Yet that office told my defense lawyers that the notes were destroyed, all of them. Then the state turned them over to us two weeks before the trial.

The state still had evidence out on October 4, just as the trial was about to begin. They hadn't even taken my tissue samples until May 24. None of them had matched anything found at the crime scene.

Prossnitz's closing statement summed up the false, misleading, and downright wrong arguments the prosecution had pushed during the trial.

Think about two people you dearly love, he told the jury. *How could anybody force you to confess to their murders, even if you'd been up all night? Why would he confess? Because police were allowing him to get it off his chest. You can con people, but it's almost impossible to fake emotion. The guilt came rushing out.*

Davies told the jury that the detectives "spoon-fed" information for my "confession." *Could any of you sit in that chair for twenty-four hours and think you were free to go when there are police officers on either side of you?*

Prossnitz dismissed all that, saying I had set up the "con" from the start, and pretended to act crazy by saying I heard voices and speaking in Spanish, continuing through the night when I talked about my "vegetables and wheelbarrow."

He tried to act crazy, Prossnitz said. *But he's crazy like a fox.*

Contradicting the pathologist's testimony, he told the jury that the knife police found in my parents' kitchen was physical evidence of my guilt. *The shape of that handle, whether it is straight or whether it is a folded buck knife, it is that knife type handle. What was the signature wound on Ruth Gauger's skull, that racetrack shape. That is the signature wound of this case. No physical evidence? He says he used a buck-type knife. Buck-type knives are not only capable of cutting a throat but it fits that wound on her skull like a key in a lock,* he said.

Prossnitz brought home his argument in a question that never should have been allowed. He wondered out loud why I kept silent after the interrogation had ended at ten thirty A.M. Saturday, when I realized I needed a lawyer. Prossnitz wanted to know why didn't I say, "Wait a second, there is no physical evidence against me, you don't have anything against me, you just have this hypothetical statement." *Why doesn't he protest it? Why doesn't he protest it? Because he confessed and in his heart of hearts it is the truth,* he told the jury.

So much for *Miranda* rights.

After all the witnesses had testified at trial, after the prosecution's and our closing statements, Prossnitz brought in an unannounced new witness: Deputy Sheriff Joy Patnaude, who had booked me into the jail the morning charges were filed against me. Prossnitz never gave us the chance to respond to her testimony, which claimed I told her I had an alcoholic blackout the day before. My own lawyers couldn't even question her. Couldn't bring up the fact that I hadn't had a drink in weeks. Even if they could have responded, though, the fact remains that the state broke the rules concerning discovery, because they never gave us any notice that a new witness was going to be added. The first time we heard any of her testimony—or even heard she was going to be called—was that morning, in the courtroom, on the last day of the trial.

Did Cowlin see it our way? Not surprisingly, he sided with Prossnitz. And he said he just wanted to get the whole thing over with—the "thing" being my trial—and into the hands of the jury.

The jury was out less than three and a half hours. I was still convinced I was going to be freed, right until the jury foreman read the guilty verdict. The lawyers had told me that the longer the jury took to deliberate, the better my chances would be. I had barely gotten back to my cell when I was told the verdict was in. After the guilty verdict was read, my attorney talked to the jury foreman. He said that up until the last day, he had been inclined to vote not guilty, but he just could not understand how anyone—even after twenty-two hours of interrogation—could confess to a crime he didn't commit. And they just couldn't believe that three veteran police officers would get on the stand and lie.

Davies admitted to us he hadn't planned to win the trial, although he *was* laying down a good groundwork for appeal on the basis of false arrest. Cowlin said during the trial that the police had plenty of reasons to arrest me, but the detectives argued both sides, also saying they *didn't* arrest me. The judge said if I wasn't under arrest, it was okay, but if I was, it wouldn't matter. That was the prosecution's argument, and he went with it.

AT MY SENTENCING HEARING in January, Ginger had the difficult job of putting into words the impact that my parents' murders and my conviction had on our family.

. . .[We] suffered the loss of our parents, and we're still suffering the pain and anguish caused by the imprisonment of my brother, Gary Gauger, whom I believe to be innocent. I feel that an incomplete investigation was done and the murderer is still at large. . . . My parents loved the farm and their family. And it was their dream that Gary would continue to farm it. Prosecution and a misguided attempt at justice has destroyed their dream. All my dreams are gone, also, with the exception of one. That the truth comes out and Gary is released.

I was sentenced to die by lethal injection.

Letters, 1994

I MET NICKI AND STEVE NELSON at the farmstand before I even moved to Texas. They stopped by from time to time after I got back, too. Before that, the Nelsons knew my dad. Steve got his first British bike in 1971 and my dad was the go-to guy for parts. They bought a Triumph about a decade later, and Nicki recalled that my mom once gave them terrific advice on how to fix a perplexing problem with the bike. Even so, I honestly couldn't put the name with the face for a while after Nicki started writing to me.

When they heard about my arrest, they told me later, they instinctively felt something was very wrong with the police's conclusion about who killed my parents. After my death sentence was announced, Nicki asked Lars Anderson if he thought I'd like to have some letters. He said I would like that very much, and told Nicki how to go about writing to the jail.

She wrote the first letter in January 1994. I wrote back, and our letters became a lifeline.

◆ FEBRUARY

Dear Nicki,

An article in our church prison newspaper estimates that one in ten Illinois prisoners is innocent and should not be in jail. And then Illinois cuts its public appeal staff by ten percent. I guess prisoners don't have any political clout. That's one of the things I'm hoping will come out of all this—that an extreme case like this may make people more aware that situations like this exist. I know I never paid much attention to it. One of the arguments the prosecutor used at my trial was that the detectives who testified against me weren't like police in Chicago or Los Angeles; they were cops you'd see shopping at Kmart or Farm and Fleet. It really made me sick. People don't want to believe they have police who would lie over issues like this. I didn't believe it. I trusted Hendle and Lowery. If I hadn't, none of this would have happened.

I called the appellate defender's office yesterday. They have some papers Ginger faxed over and they said they'd get started on them. I'm really glad. The sooner things get started, the sooner I get out. This early start could knock three to six weeks (or more) off the time I spend in jail. Believe me, on a day-by-day basis three weeks is a lot. At least I feel something is being done. When I heard everything was being held up because the transcript typist took a vacation . . . well, stuff like that is hard on me. The court . . . process . . . moves . . . so . . . slowly. I feel like I'm caught in a black hole where time and space are distorted and no light can escape.

It sounds like your trip down to Northwestern University Law School was worth it. But Ginger says Larry Marshall, the professor who has worked on cases like this, doesn't have time to take *my* case—he must be inundated with requests from people like me who want his legal help. Did you come up with any other leads? Ginger, you, Sue, Lars . . . it's so great you went to Chicago to try to find help for me. Especially in such a bad snowstorm. There's got to be someone out there other than Davies who will see what happened to me and get me out of here. I went to court February 22 and found out that *everything is postponed until May 2!* From what I can see, that means more time in here. I found out that the average time for an appeal is *twenty months*. I thought I would be out in eight to ten months.

Lars and Sue stopped by today. It's really hard for me to accept help like this, but hey, I need it. I really do appreciate all you are doing for me. Lars talked about going over all the stuff Prossnitz said. He was so out of line and this stuff may come back to haunt them.

––––––––––

I TRY TO KEEP THE FACT that I'm locked up out of my mind. It's kind of like living in a very messy house. On one level I can function and pretend it's not there, but it's really hard to completely ignore or work around it. You really are a great writer and I love the way you express yourself. I feel fortunate I have someone like you who is willing to invest time and talent to try to make a difference here. I'm still numb and can't tell what's right and what's wrong with what's happening.

I see people (we have quite a few federal prisoners in here) who seem to have no problem with robbing someone with a gun, and I would guess killing them if necessary. A lot of local gang people. They act like being a gangster and leading the "straight up" life of a criminal is okay. It's really hard for me to fathom. Most everyone in here seems like such a nice, regular person. But there's such a lack of basic morality. Things I take for granted I don't think some of these guys ever learned.

I got out of bed around six forty-five this morning and the sun was already way up, and it finally dawned on me: Spring is here and I'm missing it. I know I shouldn't let circumstances get to me, but sometimes this all seems so unnecessary. Then I look at the bigger picture and realize perhaps it is. I've always wanted to do something to help the world, but being a victim of injustice never seemed part of any plan.

Sometimes the depression just washes over me. I can't make it go away. I can't attack it, can't confront it. There doesn't seem to be any way to deal with it. *I just sit here.* Man! I can't even imagine what the conclusion will be.

God, give me patience to accept where I am and the knowledge to know what I should do. Why am I in jail? What's the point? I'm really grateful that this case is so obvious that the truth will come to light eventually. What about people who are falsely convicted where it's not so obvious? What if the police had "planted" a little evidence? What if the police had been correct on their assessment of the murders and the "confession" *did* match the crime? Ultimately that is the one thing that really stands out. The "confession" is completely false in terms of what really happened, but it mirrors exactly what the cops knew at that time.

◆ MARCH 5

Hey! Today is my one-year birthday. One full year without an alcoholic drink. And it's Saturday, one of the better TV days. This pod has enough sophistication to watch nature shows. We watched *Explorer* this morning, an episode about some crazy guys who went to the North and South poles so they could freeze their feet and eyeballs and almost die in the process. What drives some people?

Ginger left me some commissary money. It's been three weeks since I've gotten any amount of commissary junk food. I feel better without it, but the short-term buzz helps me forget where I'm at for a little while. If I'm smart I'll buy a sketchpad and a bunch of envelopes and shampoo and stuff, instead of just sugar and chocolate. I never ate candy on the outside.

I don't know if the appellate defender staff is spending much time going over my case or not. I sure hope this doesn't just put everything on hold for another two months. Anyway, I want to put together some sort of letter seeing if there isn't some way to speed things up. Perhaps I should just put together a list of questions and give them a call.

Ginger wants me to get a copy of the jury selection transcripts. Last time I tried to get transcripts the guards shot me down, but I'm ready to try again. The appellate defender takes collect call from me, but the calls are at least seven dollars each so I want to have something to say. Sometimes I have trouble believing what has happened so far. It's really hard to explain brainwashing to people who have never had it done to them. Your thinking changes after long hours of isolation and constant indoctrination. It's still very unpleasant for me and I only review it superficially unless I really *have* to explore it in any depth.

I can also see where chronic drunkenness left me more vulnerable to these forces. That's one reason I'm so grateful I was sober for five weeks when all this happened. God, what if I'd have been drunk on Thursday? I would still possibly believe what the police said.

I'm taking all this from a *very* self-centered position of what it means to *me* and what I have to do to help myself *get out of here!* Or is that completely beyond me now? And if so, what's the value of prayer? It's hard for me when I pray—believing that it will work—and nothing seems to happen. I asked about this at church service last Sunday and was told to wait. So here I sit.

On a very real level I have to accept that Hendle, Lowery, and I are one. Also my parents' killer or killers. That thought puts a big knot in my stomach. I have a real hard time with it. I see Dale next door here every day and I wonder, is he the one who did it? These are very real lessons I'm getting on judgment, false accusation, and forgiveness. All three lessons are wrapped in one face I see everyday, and I don't know the answer.

Let me tell you the story about Dale and Rob. I've known Rob since the end of June. We've been in four different pods since then and have become casual friends, playing cards and chess and eating together. After my conviction we were in PC together, where he learned about my case and situation.

Later, we were in GP together when Dale's face made the TV news—he was accused of killing a girl from Crystal Lake. I mentioned to Rob that I knew him. I got to thinking about it and told

Rob the next day that Dale could be my parents' killer. I was moved out in a couple days, and in a week or two Dale was moved into the same pod as Rob.

Rob does have a tendency to exaggerate. Also, Rob's parents are from Crystal Lake and he talked over both of our cases with them. Apparently some other people are also wondering if there is a connection between Dale and my parents.

Rob was talking to someone else about my case and said the police were linking Dale to my parents' murders and closing in on him. The fellow Rob was talking to motioned to him to let him know Dale was right behind them at the next table and had heard what Rob said.

The next morning Dale tried to cut his throat. Rob freaked out and wrote up his previous conversation on a request form and gave it to a guard. The guard took it, read it, and came back later, very interested in knowing if Rob felt he had contributed to Dale's attempted suicide.

Rob told me about this when he was moved into this pod about ten days ago. I was interested, but never got the name of the fellow Rob talked to or the name of the guard. I figured Rob would be in here until May and that I had lots of time for details. Anyway, the next day Rob got moved out of the pod for fighting, so I haven't had a chance to get more information.

This could be very significant, or it could just be a red herring. I doubt if the police want to make a connection between Dale and my parents. But then there's also the unsolved murder down Clark Road four or five years ago. That was very similar to the murder in Crystal Lake.

Ginger just bought a book, *Gone in the Night*, about the murder of a young girl in the south Chicago suburbs about six years ago. Her parents were charged and her father convicted on no real evidence. It apparently got a lot of media attention. The similarities between that case and mine are incredible. I told Ginger to get the book because it may give her ideas of contacts to tap or at least give her an idea of the process I still may have to go through.

I go from thinking logically about my situation to ranting and raving. Fuck the cops. *Let me out of here! Man!* This pisses me off sometimes. I wonder if I'll ever be at peace again. I run a chronic level of dissatisfaction in here. To be *fulfilled* again, I need patience, patience. Still haven't meditated. I must be going nuts.

I TRIED TO TALK TO EVAN A LITTLE ABOUT FARMING. Damn. It's just so hard to farm from jail. My ideas about farming are about 180 degrees opposite Evan's, but what can I say from here in jail? We're back to the classic discussion/argument I used to always have with my dad about a hay crop. To me you're just selling off the top-soil for money. And you don't even make any money on a hay crop. So frustrating. At times like this it's really hard to forgive Hendle and Lowery. It's an ongoing process that never seems to end. I just want to eat about eight candy bars and space out for awhile. Let go of attachments! I see the lesson. I wonder how long I have to beat myself up before I learn it.

◆ SUNDAY NIGHT

THEY ALWAYS SEEM TO FEED US REAL LIGHTLY on Sunday. I suspect it's so we're inspired to order more commissary. Someone has a good deal going—the stuff is *way* overpriced. I ordered a bunch of chocolate again so I can blank out for a couple of days. I really need to fast, but there's nothing to break it with when it's over and then I'm hungry for weeks afterward. I got extra fruit instead of cake and cookies—I talked them into thinking I'm hypoglycemic to get that. Actually, I may very well be. I also think I'm sensitive to wheat flour, but there's no avoiding that in here short of a full-blown allergic reaction. I don't feel good after eating sugar or white flour. Oh well, we all have our crosses to bear.

Well, got through your letter, called Ginger and Evan, wrote another letter. Now all I have to do is get my taxes off and I would have had a good day. Yes, I still have to file taxes even if I'm in jail. Shouldn't be too hard this year. My mom always used to help me with them. Damn! Reality check! Seems like about every day something reminds me of something else, and I shudder. Sometimes it passes, sometimes it doesn't.

I am very impressionable and susceptible to what people tell me. That's one reason the cops had such an easy time with me, especially considering the circumstances. They really took advantage of me, and I still have a hard time accepting where they were coming from to do that. I suppose that's one reason I'm so shy. People can hurt me. I make myself vulnerable and it hurts when that trust is betrayed.

If Hendle and Lowery are human at all, they must be really rationalizing, denying, and suppressing what happened the night of the interrogation. Lowery not so much—he came across as an idiot and a buffoon—but Hendle! She was so sincere, so believable. I just couldn't comprehend anyone in her position lying like she did. And then to continue it by lying to the grand jury. I have a hard time with that. I think now they're just keeping it all going to save their own asses. They will ultimately have to face the truth, but I don't know when. Reminds me of a little kid who breaks something and then hides the pieces and lies about it, doesn't it? But then so did the Iran-Contra deal. We've got some little kids in some very powerful places.

Intellectually I accept being in here most of the time now. But I look out the window and wonder when I'll be out and what it will feel like. My attorney talks in terms of years. I just can't accept that.

Just these last four weeks, with the post-trial motion postpone-
ments, seemed to go on forever. I'm a slow-growing seed right now.
Or a seventeen-year locust. Just a grub on a root, waiting to
emerge.

IT'S A NICE DAY, so I thought I'd run through some gardening
tips. Do you have a decent shovel? A hoe? Get your shovel and
sharpen its digging edge. Do you have a grinding wheel? If it's
rusty, clean it. If the handle is old, oil it. Same for your hoe.

To get rid of the grass in the cold frame, just dig out the sod,
knock a little dirt off of it and use the sod around the bottom of
the cold frame and anywhere there's a hole. Taking out the grass
will help because the frame is not very tall and you'll get a couple
more inches. Buy yourself a bale of peat moss. Spade up the ground
after the sod is removed. Break up the chunks. Once the dirt is
nicely broken up, add some rabbit shit and at least half the bale of
peat moss. Add some sand, too, about a bag or bucket full. Mix this
up real well. If you have a half-inch hardware screen, screening the
dirt *is* better, but not absolutely necessary.

At this point you should have a nice seedbed. It it's dry from
the peat moss, water it and let it sit until you're ready to use it. Now
you can start seeding your lettuce, flowers, and spinach. Be sure to
plant them in rows, six to twelve inches apart, depending on how
much transplanting you plan on doing, and mark the rows. This
way it will be easy to run a hoe down the rows once the plants start
to sprout. Even in a cold frame, it's a good idea to cultivate.

Let's talk about hardening plants off. The plants you started
inside should be hardened off before you transplant them. All you
have to do is move them in their containers and let them live out
in the cold frame for about a week.

This way, it's still possible to move the plants back inside in
case of unseasonably cold or freezing weather. After the first week

in April, it usually doesn't get cold enough to freeze through a cold frame. I cover the frame in the evening if it gets cold, but we're talking temperatures way below freezing here. For me it's instinctive, but until you get a feel for it, it's hard to say exactly. This all seems so simple to me, but I think back and remember all that I had to do to develop this system.

Get an idea of inside temperatures during the day. You want to try to keep temperatures from going much over 100 or 110 degrees. It's not much of a problem yet but will be in a few weeks. Basically, between eleven A.M. and four P.M. on bright sunny days there is a danger of cooking the plants in the cold frame and you will have to open it up. Until it gets warmer, it doesn't take much of an opening to moderate the heat. It's simple but does require daily attention. Close the frames around four P.M. to store up the afternoon heat. I know I can get borderline compulsive about running cold frames, but I had one behind my mom's kitchen that she watched and it doesn't have to be all that complicated.

I'm feeling kind of weird this afternoon. Last year is coming back to me in a very real way. Foods featured in the newspaper ads, Easter, the warm weather, and gardening. It's really hard for me to relate to Bev Hendle and Eugene Lowery today.

P.S. April 1, morning—the guards are right at it. They got everyone up for breakfast and then it didn't come for twenty-five minutes. Ha! April Fools! Next they'll probably have a shakedown. Perhaps they'll give us baked potatoes and no salt again. That's *always* funny.

◆ APRIL

SO THE CENSORS TOOK the letter to the editor I sent you. Too bad—it was a good one. It was written by one of the defense attorneys from two of Rolando Cruz's trials. I thought it was significant that he gave his name and listed (the Loop) as his address. I was wondering if the *Sun-Times* would give us his address. The letter to the editor was in the fifth column of the editorials around March 23. Anyway, think there's any point in pursuing it, or do you think that's covered with the contacts you guys made at Northwestern?

I'm sending another article about a man wrongfully convicted of a 1980 murder in Oak Park. Apparently quite a large Christian coalition sprang up to support his release and I was wondering if we could tap into that. The article says he's reemerging in the public eye with a book he's just had published (*Maximum Security* by Steven Linscott). It might lead to a good source of contacts. What do you think?

While we're clearing up old business, do you think the Rob thing is worth pursuing? I wrote him and asked for the name of the guard he talked to and the name of the person he talked to, but haven't gotten a reply. Either he's not answering or he never got the letter. Something of interest: Rob's in the next pod over. "Special Needs." Same pod Dale is in. A stab of paranoia. What if Rob and Dale are cooking up something? Why is Rob over there? This is the kind of thing you think about when you're in here.

You said your letter to the *Herald* got people wondering. Any chance of me getting a copy? Wait until people start seeing all this stuff being put together in a complete way.

CALLED GINGER AND EVAN last night. The discussion didn't seem to go anywhere. Ginger is of the opinion that if there was another trial the verdict would be the same. I just don't see how that's possible. Who's being the stubborn one here? Ginger and Bill Davies insist a retrial would do no good. To me it's so obvious. What am I missing here? I heard the jury instructions. We argued about that a little, and when that wasn't going anywhere I asked what they planned to do about farming. That was even less productive. No one listens to what I say. Am I that far off base? It makes no sense for Evan to try to farm like he's planning to. He'll work most of the spring and half the summer on it and possibly make a thousand bucks gross while running down the land (not building it up, anyway). I can just start ranting on this. We can waste $100,000 on a lawyer I never wanted, against my suggestions and thinking, who did me little good, yet we can't spend $200 to $300 and give up $350 from land rent for one year to build up the soil and make it easier on everybody.

I'll be so glad when someone else gets a hold of this case. I hate to argue with Ginger and Evan. I could possibly beat Ginger down with arguments until she gave in, but it's just not that important. Ginger's going to talk to the family attorney today and they're coming tonight. I could just let Evan go ahead and try to put in a corn crop, but it seems like such a waste of effort and time for the little they would get back.

Ginger is of the opinion that my stuff (tractors, bikes, cars, equipment, Grandpa's house) will have to be sold because my ex-wife's attorneys are pushing for quick liquidation of my estate for my kids. (The state takes the position that I'm already dead.) I'm trying not to be attached to material goods, but I've cut loose of so much in my life, I've started over from scratch so many times. Is this what God's telling me? Do I have to let it all go? Or is this where I have to learn to be strong and really stand up for what I want? A lot of this stuff is irreplaceable. Which makes it priceless, right? It's not stuff that has a lot of monetary value, but it's really *me*. It's taken years of going through stuff to decide on what I really want. There is an old MGB. It's nothing much, but it's sound and runs well. I've even got a spare motor for it that only has 14,000 miles on it. I've saved that motor for twenty-five years and finally have a place to put it. Tractors, old horse-drawn farm equipment. Stuff that's perfect for vegetables.

It seems like my brother is pushing for a quick sale, too. Break up the motorcycle business, get rid of stuff my dad and his father spent a lifetime putting together. It serves no one to force a quick sale. My brother and my kids don't need the money. If we hold on to the property for a couple of years, a controlled sale will be worth so much more. It's insane. The rationale must be, if it's bad for me and Ginger, it must be good for them. We'll see. Damn! It just never seems to stop. I know ultimately everything will work out, but I don't want to regret decisions for the rest of my life that I make here, either. Actually at this point I personally don't seem to be allowed much along the lines of decision making. As I've said, the state looks at me like I'm already dead. (That's funny! I didn't even know I was sick!)

To me it seems like a simple thing to put together a presentation showing what a lousy case the state has against me and getting a court injunction to stop things until this all gets sorted out. Ginger, however, has taken the position that the law's the law and it can't be stopped. Nothing even starts to happen with my appeal until after May 2 as far as I can see. I'm going to call Bill Davies before then to make sure there are no other stalling tricks the county can come up with to slow the appeal.

———————

Gauger Trial Questioned

To the editor:

With April here, I am reminded of the ongoing cruelties inflicted on the family of Ruth and Morrie Gauger.

A year ago, the Gaugers were murdered at their rural Richmond home. And while the sheriff's department considers this case closed, many in Richmond believe that today the wrong man—the couple's son Gary—sits in jail, wrongfully sentenced to die.

In a trial which boasted not a single piece of forensic evidence, the prosecution's contention was that Gary Gauger inexplicably, out of a clear blue sky, "snapped" one morning and murdered the parents he so loved.

To support their claim, prosecutors brought forth no evidence, called no eyewitnesses, in fact, never even managed to come up with a motive. Instead, they relied on what they liked to refer to as a "confession"—a statement exacted during a grueling 20-hour interrogation of the Gaugers' son, which began shortly after Gary discovered his father's body.

Convinced he was not upset enough, not crying enough, officers began telling Gary that he must be the murderer, having somehow "blocked out the memory."

Upset and exhausted, yet trying throughout the all-night interrogation to be cooperative and having been convinced that such an exercise would reveal whether any information was "buried in his subconscious," Gary agreed to concoct a hypothetical scenario as to "how he would have killed his parents, if he had actually done it."

What is most amazing about the statement which followed—which officers would later dub "a confession," is that the description of the crime, as Gary imagined it, was not even the same as the method of death later revealed by the official autopsy!

I suggest the people of Richmond make their homes more secure and keep their doors locked. This murder, added to the unsolved homicide on Clark Road (about a mile from the Gauger home), does not lend this community much peace of mind.

Nicola A. Nelson
Richmond, Ill.

NICKI, YOUR LETTER to the editor exceeded my wildest expectations. I'm overwhelmed! You can't imagine what it's like. I'm starting to feel again. I'm hanging on to my desk, breathing hard, trying to write, brushing back tears. I'm starting to shake. I'm laughing. I can't thank you enough. It's out there—someone has finally said something. What a rush. Real feelings!

I agree with what you wrote to me—the police do have a stressful, dangerous job, and it isn't really any wonder some of them get loopy. That's been one of my points. The Brown's Chicken thing was fresh in everyone's minds. The Cumbe case was coming to trial and Hendle and Lowery were under a lot of pressure to implicate him in that, and then POW—another one. I can see where their judgment could have been off, but then, that cover up. Fudging the notes, lying to the grand jury. That's where they really blew it.

The *Sun-Times* did a telephone poll asking whether the 156 or so people on death row should be executed. Ninety percent of the people who phoned in said yes. My role in all this is becoming clearer all the time. I suppose I should consider it an honor to be chosen to do the work. Believe me, there is still work for me in here. I suppose if my faith were stronger, it would be easier. It bothers me most that I'm wasting time. Not fulfilling my dreams.

I TOOK A LITTLE TIME OFF from letter writing and reading and got involved in some heavy card playing with some of the fellow peas in the pod. Not very constructive, but it's fun and helps the time pass. A few of us in here now are of a similar age and background, so I can actually relate a little with some of these guys. The next couple of weeks will probably be my last chance for much human interaction for a while. It looks like I'll be going to Menard, wherever that is, and be in segregation for twenty-two hours a day. (This is just speculation on my part). I should be here for at least two more weeks, probably three. It usually takes a couple weeks for your paperwork to precede you before you're shipped.

Ginger and Evan were here last night. I guess our family lawyer is under some pressure from Ronda's to wrap things up on the estate. We talked about various things, but nothing really got decided. It looks to me like Ginger is getting tired of everything and just wants to go along with whatever the attorney says. I feel so cut off from everything. I'll just reserve judgment until after May 2. I really only have partial information and half-formed ideas on anything right now.

I've gotten away from Bible study, Bible reading, and church. Kind of let myself "go" these last couple months. If I try to keep my energy levels where I think they should be, and do the stuff suggested in various books, I build up expectations. Then I get the letdown, which leaves me disillusioned and discouraged. I really don't think the roller coaster ride is where it's at. It seems self-destructive to me. But if I just hang out and try to flow, I seem to sink into discouragement and become bewildered. I'm really at a loss what role I'm supposed to play in all this. I seem to be the central figure in a drama that has nothing to do with me. It's strange. I really want to get something out of all this, but my efforts seem so futile and irrelevant. There just seem to be locked doors (literally) everywhere I turn.

What a bunch of shit about the Cruz case in those articles. Okay, now we're getting down to the beans and tortillas. It seems like the police and prosecutors use a standard handbook for setting people up and railroading them, doesn't it?

———

◆ MAY

MAY 2, COURT DAY: Everything has been put on hold again! Man! Well, at least if it's not a neck-and-neck race with Ronda's attorney about which comes first, my acquittal or the estate settlement, I don't have to suffer such a feeling of urgency and frustration of time passing. Now delays are merely more time little ol' me spends rotting in a jail cell.

At this point the principal suspects seem to be: some unknown motorcycle person (robbery); a paid hit man (some real estate person my parents wouldn't sell to); D.M. (he lost his house back to my parents); Dale (a local, supposedly a murderer, knew my parents); the fellow who found my dad with me — he lost some money on a bike deal and my dad was holding the bike; or even my brother. Although he is acting very strange, that theory seems absurd to me. What a list, huh? It's too bad we can't count on any sort of police support or investigation.

I still wonder what that business of the police never taking fingerprints was all about. Other possible suspects could have been implicated by matching prints. The police spent over 3,000 hours, I heard, investigating the crime scene but they never dusted the garage or rug shop doorknob for prints.

I talked to Ginger and Evan last night. She's going to ask Bill Davies to talk to Paul Barrett, the lawyer who's taking care of the estate business. Apparently Paul still thinks I'm guilty and is moving to have the estate settled. Poor Ginger, stuck in the middle of all this. We got to talking about that and my brother and my lack of confidence in Bill Davies. Ginger thinks Davies is going a great job. My last chance to fire him was really back last June — 20/20 hindsight!

Anyway, it didn't take long to get both Ginger and Evan hollering at me. Apparently I've managed to incur a fair share of resentment over the years. It's really hard for me to explain my position and thought process over the years. Especially to someone who never drank. Especially in a limited phone conversation.

As a person, Davies seems like a nice man. I like Russ, too. They just don't seem to see things like I do. Also, Davies is evasive. And one time he tried to slip me a quit claim deed for my interest in any Illinois property. He had me sign away my interest in the property I had in Wisconsin and told me I needed to sign two forms because of the way the property is divided. That part is true—the property is in two different sections. The first page was clearly labeled, "Wisconsin, Trempelow County." The second page looked the same but was covered by a piece of paper except where I was supposed to sign. This was on the morning he was to give closing arguments and we were talking about other things. He acted like it was almost sort of an afterthought. Anyway, I almost signed both copies, but then looked at the second page more closely and saw that it was a blank quit claim deed form for *Illinois*. He could have typed in anything he wanted to later. I asked him about it and he said, "Oh, they must have sent me the wrong form." But come on. He made up a story about having to sign two forms, he covered the writing of the second form and tried to get me to sign it when I was distracted. Things like that do not inspire confidence in the man. I'm sure he's destroyed the deed, or else he may stick to the wrong-form story, but I just can't seem to trust him any more.

I really want to get this out of his hands. He's also been very evasive on cost beforehand, and then floored me once it was too late to fire him. It's no accident that most of our lawmakers were lawyers first, and it's no accident that they profit from the system they've set up.

I suppose I should make a will in case I get killed in jail or something. Man, I never considered anything like that. I'd just always assumed if I died everything would go to my kids. I suppose I should ask Ginger about it. It's just something our family never talked about. Most of the stuff I own now really doesn't mean much to anyone but me. My '71 Triumph is about my most prized possession. I paid $400 for that bike. I should do something, I suppose, to help try to keep the homestead together in case something happened to me. My attorney already has everything that's worth much money. I'll probably end up taking the same path my parents took and just let stuff happen as it will.

———

WOKE UP PARANOID THIS MORNING, wondering if my lawyers or Ronda's family or some developers are setting me up for something else. Well, I'm sick of stewing in my own juices again so I guess I'll pick up my pencil and write to you. I can apparently only isolate within myself for so long before thoughts start ricocheting around inside my head like a BB in a toy rattle.

Last week in court. The guards won't let me talk to anyone in the gallery. I guess I could turn around and make faces or stare. Actually, they've also stopped me before when I've done that.

I wonder why all of a sudden the shackles.

I really appreciate the card you sent me. For one thing, the picture reminded me of my dad's woods in the spring. Also your news on the papers' coverage of the latest developments was very enlightening to me. I had taken a completely negative attitude of the latest developments. It did, I assume, open people's eyes to the fact that this is anything but an open-and-shut case.

It's been eight months since my conviction, and it doesn't look like anything has even gotten started yet. I really want to get this out of Davies's and Cowlin's hands. I can't see anything happening as long as this stays in McHenry County. I'm going to call Davies this week, but he never clarifies anything for me. Seeing through the glass darkly.

———

So you think I should write a gardening book? It's crossed my mind, but I always figured it had all been done before. I guess I do have a different philosophy about gardening, though. I like to keep costs to an absolute minimum, emphasize recycling (organic and inorganic materials), and maximize the seasons, a person's labor, the variety, and enjoyment.

Perhaps my books could gain a cult following like John Wayne Gacy's paintings. The state has all these people on death row—it's an untapped resource! Death row jewelry, artwork, greeting cards. Think of the potential!

Our pod is rapidly being taken over by kids. I like to watch cartoons now and again—you know, the classics: old Popeye, Merry Melody, Bugs Bunny, but these guys! I expected to see *My Pretty Pony* on next. They're preschoolers! Fun on a Saturday night usually consists of arguing about what we're going to watch on TV. Unless it's a good movie everyone wants to watch (and keep quiet through) it's almost impossible to follow the dialog anyway, so I suppose you could look at the argument as the high point and the rest as anticlimax.

———

I'm in a little better mood this morning. Looks like showers are on the way. I see they've put in four apple trees here on the north corner of the lawn. Kind of a strange choice, I would think, especially for a windbreak. Oh well, the blossoms are pretty. I can't imagine anyone ever eating the apples. Who's to say what will be happening around here in twenty to sixty years? It takes a good fifteen years for an apple tree to really produce anything, unless they've put in dwarfs.

Well, *I was* in a good mood. It's like a dark cloud passed through my mind when I started thinking about the apple trees. I started a dozen apple trees from seed about eighteen years ago and planted them along my dad's property line. He kept them pruned and we got our first decent crop off them the fall of 1992. These apples are all crossed with each other from apples we'd gotten from Ronda's grandmother's orchard, so none of the varieties are recognizable, but they're all good, firm, winter-keeping cider apples.

I've fallen into a routine of reading and playing spades. Not too productive, but it's rather pleasant and the time is passing. But on the other hand, I don't want to just pass the time. I mean, this *is* my life.

Can't bring myself to meditate. I used to meditate last spring, when the injustice of my reality seemed intolerable, but now that I've acquired a degree of acceptance, I'm afraid to change my routine for fear of bringing those feelings back.

I've pretty much quit writing in my journal, too. These letters accomplish the same purpose and at least I have a letter in the mail when I'm done. I've sporadically kept writings and journals since my divorce as a record of my state of mind, with the idea of reviewing them at a later date to see if I've progressed in any way. Of course, the police seized all of that, and even wanted to use my AA fourth-step work against me at the trial. I can see them taking a phrase here, half a sentence there, and admitting it as more damning evidence. For one reason or another, they didn't do it. Not that there was anything in it to use. Anything they used would have had to be used completely out of context to be any good to them. That's probably why they didn't. To read my writing in its entirety would demonstrate my absence of malice. The stuff on my ex-wife under the "resentments" heading was quite extensive, but so what?

So some guy in Iowa is talking about being the murderer now. It sounds farfetched but I can't dismiss it. But this type of investigation is police business and it's going to take a mandate from the state, not the county, I'm afraid, to reopen the case. There I go again, acting like I know what's going on. You'd think I'd know better by now. Sometimes I want to cry, sometimes I want to pray, and sometimes I just want to sleep. What a life.

————

GINGER WROTE TO ME Monday, trying to get info on tracking down Rob. She finally decided that the issue was relevant, I guess. Anyway, we were having trouble locating his parents so we could ask them to contact him about the names of the people he spoke with. I got some leads from another inmate and I hope Ginger and Evan will be able to get what we need from Rob in case it's ever needed for an investigation.

There's a new guy in here who plays chess. We're fairly evenly matched and he's into playing three to six games a day so it keeps me occupied. I'm getting a little tired of spades. A group of guys wants to play my partner and me for commissary, but they cheat. I could cheat too, I suppose, but I'm not sure if I can count on my partner to pick it up. Is it moral? Is this a test of my cosmic morality or just psychological melodrama on my part? Sometimes I'm amazed at the trivial garbage I occupy my mind with.

It's hard to get too close to anyone in here. It just seems like an endless string of bad news and trouble, and there's really not much you can do for a person but listen. I guess I can do that. There are some straight-up crooks and dangerously violent people in here, but so many just don't seem to be able to quite fit in the mold cast for them. I suppose a little discipline and polishing is probably good for all of us. A lack of discipline and respect for authority seems to be a common denominator for a lot of us in here.

I've always taken an ambivalent attitude toward the death penalty. I vaguely knew it was wrong, but figured that as long as warfare, "police actions," and abortion were legal and encouraged, any strong position on capital punishment was moot. I've since taken a closer look at it—not much choice—and see it as a venge-ful act that serves no constructive purpose. Considering that the people who actually implement the execution are not the people affected by the crime, I really wonder what their true motives are. Just want to kill someone, I guess.

Ol' Prossnitz in the news. Makes you wonder what makes a guy like that tick, doesn't it? It's hard for me to imagine him taking himself seriously. I really wish the trial had been on videotape, just so people could see him in action. The other guy wasn't too bad. Just doing his job. Just stoking the furnace. But Prossnitz, man.

Well, back to real life. There have been almost two fights already tonight and you couldn't even hear the TV if you wanted to. Just a couple of different people moving in upsets the whole bal-ance, and all the borderline cases start to lose it. I've got three books I want to check out, and this looks like a good week to do some reading.

Dreams and Distress Calls

◆ June 1994

Dear Nicki,

I'm sitting around waiting for the door to open for supper. I feel like a cat sitting in the kitchen waiting for someone to open the refrigerator so I can get underfoot. Then, like a cat, as soon as they feed me I'll sniff it once and complain because it isn't something better. Then I'll eat it anyway.

Thanks for your encouragement about a retrial or a complete dismissal of the charges once the state court gets my case. I'm still afraid someone's going to throw some sort of curveball next week. I would think Hendle and Lowery would be terrified to have this case leave the county. To me, the preponderance of evidence seems to be overwhelmingly against the state. But I can see why people don't want to believe what the detectives did. It's an amazing fuckup, and the implications—to me at least—are enormous.

I feel like a political prisoner more than anything, on the receiving end of everything I don't like about Illinois politics. I suppose that's a broad overstatement—I'm sure there are countless avenues of persecution left untapped. And my situation, at least right now, is very little compared with what a large number of people in the world must endure. At least I wasn't hauled off in the middle of the night, beaten until I confessed, and hung on the spot.

The evening guards were particularly prickly last night. They tried to lock down a couple of guys for no reason other than they were playing cards too loudly. When the guys successfully stood up for themselves, the guards must have powwowed and jumped on the next chance to exert their authority. They locked down two other prisoners because one gave the other a couple of Ritz crackers from his commissary.

And I'm locked down for trading food—three days. That seems a little excessive for taking a couple of oranges off abandoned trays, and I didn't actually *trade* with anyone. I managed to get six apples yesterday, good ones, too! It's always a challenge hiding the apples during the morning search. Well, I guess I'll do some reading. I was just thinking this morning that perhaps I should get myself locked down for a couple of days to get some work done. The mind is powerful!

I love the rain showers we've been having. I remember one year I jumped the gun and beat all the other local growers by a good two weeks. I lucked out and didn't get frosted. Then around this time of year, we needed rain. Small local showers were forecast for the day, and I watched one black cloud form in the west around ten A.M. I watched it move off to the north, go around me to the east, keep moving back to the south, and at about two it moved in and opened up. We got six inches of hail and it flattened everything. We were the only farm to get hit, and it knocked me back about fifteen days. It's funny now, and I think I laughed about it a little then, too. I eventually recovered and had a good crop, but I sure lost my edge on the competition.

————

JUNE 16: Oh shit! Just got back from court. You saw it. They say July 8 is the next date anything can happen, but they're also talking about September 11. If Prossnitz and Cowlin have their way, this case will never get out of the county. Damn, this sucks. Now I won't know anything for another three weeks. Did you listen to Prossnitz today? How can he live with himself? He can't possibly believe the shit he says. I'm losing it. I've tried to be patient. Right out of three days lockdown into this. Will I ever have a life again? It's driving me crazy. I don't know whether to laugh or cry. My head hurts. I can't even talk to anyone about what's going on. And it looks like Prossnitz is using the "two cutting motions" as his main piece of evidence. That wasn't even in the early police report—it didn't appear until after the autopsy. I never heard it until the trial. They just make shit up as they go along as they need it and bury everything else under delays, doubletalk, and bullshit.

Thanks for sending me the copy of the *Northwest Herald*. The bad news was that it said an appeal after conviction takes one and a half to two years, but at least it's a confirmation of what I've been going through. It was driving me nuts thinking McHenry County was stalling and that no one seemed to notice, much less care. It explained more about the appeal process, too. It amazes me how I've been left out in the dark on all this. Davies doesn't tell me anything. Right now, the most appalling thing is the lack of investigation. After hearing the chief detective on the stand, I realize my fears are probably true—that they would suppress any breaks that *did* come along.

Just think: Davies and Miller cost me (not counting the prep work) about $2,400 for their half-day appearance in court.

I'm glad you got to see what a little weasel Prossnitz can be. Wouldn't it be something if Cowlin did the right thing and gave me a directed verdict? Who knows? It could happen. The prosecutor, judge, and state are so intent on maintaining their completely false set of "facts," though, they're like a top running on their own inertia. They're wobbling, but there's nothing to counteract them to make them stop. They sure don't seem like they can do it on their own.

———

I'VE BEEN HAVING SOME VERY REAL DREAMS lately dealing with my dad and my ex-wife—real-life stuff, working out issues. It's really made me look forward to sleeping. In one dream I spent a day helping my dad organize and arrange his bikes in the back sheds, very much like I did in real life. He was being very secretive and possessive with everything, just like he was in real life. I remember thinking, "What are you going to do when you find out you get murdered and all this is for naught?"

This was the first time I've had a dream where I knew my parents would be killed, yet the dream didn't end. I suppose I could keep the dream going because I perceived their deaths as being in the future.

One of the guards (nosy fuckers) made a comment about how long it took him to censor your last two letters. To the guards: Since you're reading this, I've just got to ask, Where do you guys get off reading people's mail? Doesn't it bother you? Just doing your job? Same excuse as the guards used in Nazi Germany.

◆ JULY

Dear Nicki,

That hearing really bummed me out and pissed me off. I'm sorry you had to sit through it. I'm glad Lars and Sue weren't there. I don't know why Bill Davies never challenges Prossnitz on any of the shit he spews out. Bill just blew me off when I asked about it and acted like none of it was important. Same behavior as at the trial. If I had the assistance of a decent attorney to catch legal points and keep the trial on track, I know I could have done a better job defending myself. Although, as Hunter S. Thompson said in *Fear and Loathing in Las Vegas:* "As your attorney, I advise you to get a new lawyer."

I've made a list of some things you can do to help—if you want to. These are *suggestions*, not orders. Someone has to get the transcripts from Bill. I imagine that will have to be Ginger and Evan. I'll send a list of what I feel is important to copy—to get it done at the courthouse would cost $3,000 or more so I feel it is worth the trouble of doing it ourselves. We need the original police reports released on June 15, especially the one dealing with my "confession," and another with the names of two other officers who took part in the interrogation. I've asked Davies repeatedly to produce them, but he ignores me. It corroborates my testimony and points out a lie Pandre told on the stand when he said no other officers were involved in the interrogation. It's too late to have anything to do with the trial, but it does support my argument that Davies was incompetent. I've got to fight that fight, too.

It's so frustrating how the police lied and set me up and have since conspired to cover up the truth, yet neither of my lawyers could grasp the details or put them together to present the arguments in an orderly, convincing way. And then at this last hearing, Russ said what a good cop Lowery is and how he didn't want to imply anything or insult the court. Whose side are they on?

———

County fair time already. Summer's half over. How time flies when you're locked in a cage. Or as frogs say, "Time's fun when you're having flies." My attempts at media attention haven't gotten very far. I wrote to Channel 7, CBS, the ACLU, ABC, and a reporter from the *Sun-Times*. All I got back was a form letter from ABC's *Inside Edition* saying, "not interested, keep watching our show," and a form letter from the ACLU saying "we don't do individuals" along with a few phone numbers for legal aid.

I'm going to go ahead and send letters to the major networks. After getting letters back from the *Tribune* and *Daily Herald* I was so encouraged and ready to walk out the door. Then I reread Eric

Zorn's fourteen columns in the *Tribune* on Rolando Cruz and realized that sometimes it's not that easy. So I'll keep plugging away.

The next thing we'll hear (from local papers and the prosecution, anyway) will be "Miller and Davies are trying to get a guilty man off on technicalities." But maybe someone will look deeper. The prosecution's whole argument is that Hendle and Lowery had no way of knowing there were no signs of a defensive struggle, robbery, or forceful break-in. Hendle was out there all afternoon poking around, and Lowery got there around three. They didn't take any prints. What did they look for, if not signs of a struggle, robbery, or forced entry?

I like the way you describe Cowlin as being between a rock and a hard place. I personally think that any judge who would roll his eyes, look up at the ceiling, and turn away during the defense witness's testimony is not too concerned about public opinion, but then what do I know about the mental workings of a local judge?

To me everything hinges on getting enough public opinion to force a genuine reexamination of the case, but getting me out of this cage is also significant. Actually, I'll probably have to be released before any new examination is ever ordered. I have a hard time seeing us ever get any honest support from local authorities, especially after listening to the chief detective's testimony in June.

Wouldn't it be something if Cowlin realized his error and cut me loose? Sure would help Ginger out . . . me too! I never even considered that possibility until mid-June. Something's going to happen, so why not the *right* thing? Ginger and I have both gotten a little pessimistic about the system over the last year, but this is where I really think public pressure could have an effect.

I'm embarrassed sometimes for the less-than-charitable thoughts I've entertained toward Prossnitz, Lowery, and Hendle. That's a good lesson for me, and something tangible I can work on. I see Lowery as very confused, Hendle more frightened than anything. She seemed so honest. Prossnitz—I haven't got a clue. From a purely selfish viewpoint I see my forgiveness and enlightenment directly linked to these three. Are they all a part of me? Perhaps there is a little Prossnitz in all of us. Every time I smacked my kids when they did something I didn't want them to do. Every time I bullied my way through a situation without regard for others.

◆ AUGUST

I SAW BEVERLY HENDLE walk across the parking lot yesterday and get into a van. This forgiveness stuff is hard. My heart started racing and my blood pressure went up. I banged on the window but she didn't hear me. If she had looked up I probably would have waved or shrugged my shoulders. At least I didn't think anything bad—I just thought I should be out there and she should be in here, just to see what it's like.

I've calmed down a bunch after getting this all down on paper. I have to force myself to get some letters out. I've got addresses for shows like *Hard Copy* and *A Current Affair*, but I don't know if they'll take me seriously or if my case is too complex for TV.

I'm chomping at the bit waiting for more news or mail. I don't see how this can be ignored, but I also realize I'm just one person on a never-ending list of injustices. I mentally try to follow the path all my letters take: Guards reading it here, sealing it, sending it out. It gets sorted at the local post office and sent to Chicago. Sorted again and sent to New York. It ends up in a big office building, gets sorted with the other mail in the mailroom. Finally, a secretary in some cubicle ends up with it. Do they even get read, or are they just scanned briefly and filed in a dead letter file? I think about sending a letter saying, "Help! I've been kidnapped by political terrorists!" but I doubt that would be taken seriously, either.

I had a very profound dream last night. Our whole family— my mom, dad, brother, Ginger, and I—were getting dressed up and ready to go to court for my September appearance. As I was looking for my suit, it occurred to me: My folks could tell the judge I wasn't guilty! I went over to my mom and said, "Mom! You can tell the judge the truth! Judge Cowlin said in court that it's too bad you couldn't testify. Boy, this is going to make him look foolish!" I realized I shouldn't take such delight in making him look foolish, but I was so relieved my ordeal was going to finally be over. Then the release hit me and I was hit by a tremendous wave of emotion. I almost started howling in relief, grief, sorrow, joy. I still didn't connect with the fact that my folks were actually dead—just that somehow they could testify and things would be over. Then I started waking up . . .

Sometimes I get so far removed from the reality of this shit. It's eight A.M. now; we've already had breakfast and we're locked down, and yet in a way the dream and the intense feelings of relief and emotion still feel more real than this does.

Some people have altered their realities so badly I don't see how they will be able to accept my innocence, no matter what happens or is finally revealed. How will the prosecutor ever be able to justify the lies he told or the way he ran the trial? How about Hendle?

If we create our realities with our minds, am I really at spiritual war with these people? Is this just a reflection of the separation from God I've created myself? Is this what my perception of the universe looks like, underneath all the rationalization? If we're all one, why am I so at odds with myself? I know I'm probably my own worst enemy, but did I create all this?

———

ANOTHER REMARKABLE DREAM. I was at the farm. Ronda was there and we were working out various issues, from sex to smoking pot. We somehow activated a hologram of bike repair, with my mom and dad demonstrating how to do an emergency road strip-down of an old Triumph Twin. Then they became real and we started discussing all the old issues we had, too, mostly about making a living. It was great. The specifics aren't important, but I *knew* they were ghosts yet they didn't disappear. I could actually discuss and argue about things with my dad, and rather than him just getting mad and breaking off the conversation, he actually listened to me. They both looked *great* in their old riding outfits. They had come up with one of their old friends (another ghost) on a couple of late-'50s Triumphs. I knew they were dead and just visiting—but also that they would be back.

The last thing we talked about was getting the vegetable business going. I explained to my mom how I knew it would take three or four years to really get it up and running, and she remarked that it would probably take that long to clear up my present circumstances. At that point I realized I was still in jail, and that was enough of a shock to wake me up.

Every night I dream I'm at the farm, working with my dad. That was the one way he could really relate to us. Doing the chores, cutting wood, picking corn, making hay, fixing the buildings, putting up sheds.

The day-to-day routine was my dad's element. He liked the fluid motion of repetitive labor to get a job done. I think that's why I like hoeing, planting, and picking so much. It's so fluid. The money is in the sales presentation and merchandising, but it's the production I really like. What aspirations, huh? To be a subsistence peasant!

———————

Northwestern legal clinic: "Thanks for your letter, but we're busy." At least my mail is getting through. Got a letter from Lawrence Marshall at Northwestern last Friday—he's busy, too. I'm surprised I haven't heard from the Illinois Coalition Against the Death Penalty. I really had hoped something would have started rolling before Cowlin's ruling on our motion. I guess at this point I'll just wait until the September court date and take it from there. Got a letter from you, too. I haven't even started answering your last one. I'm so busy, what with dreams and card playing and all.

◆ SEPTEMBER

I'VE PUT OFF WRITING because everything going through my mind seems to be a complaint. I'm tired of being in here. I'm tired of waking up in here. I'm tired of the food. I'm tired of the bullshit mental exercises I give myself—they have no meaning. I'm tired of the fact that no one seems to have taken an interest in the distress calls we've sent out. That really makes me wonder. I would think this would be a great story for the news media. Has this country become such a police state that the media no longer prints anything derogatory about the police?

I mailed out a couple more letters this morning. One to a staff writer at the *Sun-Times* and another to an address Amnesty International sent me. It took three letters to Amnesty before they even responded. The last one I had smuggled out by a prisoner who was being released. A bit dramatic, perhaps, but I wasn't sure if my letters were getting out because the responses have been so slow. Is everyone on vacation? No one believes me? Everyone's understaffed and overworked? No one cares?

Those are all the notes I'm going to float until after October 22. Then I may write follow-up letters to the TV networks. I also wrote the managing editor of the *Sun-Times* last week. I had wanted to give Eric Zorn an exclusive, but he sure seems to be taking his sweet time. I realize it probably isn't possible for people to come to the rescue of every poor schmuck who gets caught up in our legal system, but I would think someone would want to consider my allegation that I ended up here after three police officers lied. It sounds pretty farfetched when I put it like that. I suppose that's my problem.

Thanks for the suggestions of good TV shows. Imagine: drama, plot, character development, and dialogue. All inappropriate qualifications for any show we watch in there. I can pretty much check off what we'll watch every night. If it's exploitative, sensationalist garbage, that's what we'll see. I used to ask, "Who would ever watch that garbage?" Instead of a poll, the TV bosses should just find out what all the idiots in jail watch — if it's a hit with the majority of the prison population, it's mainstream America!

———

THE MOST AMAZING THING happened the other day. Larry Marshall (the guy from Northwestern who had already said he was too busy to take on my case) showed up here out of the blue. I don't know if I even made any sense when I first talked to him — he said I looked like a deer in the headlights. So what I understand from him and Ginger is he was up in Madison for Yom Kippur earlier this month. He was at a service in an old synagogue there and something made him think of me. He told his assistant — maybe his girlfriend, I'm not sure — that since Woodstock was on the way back to Chicago, they should stop in and see me. I felt an immediate psychic connection with Michelle — a very good vibe coming from her. That helped me feel that this was all for the good.

I talked to Ginger last night. Larry (he prefers Larry to Lawrence) called her again. He apparently is going to start some sort of legal motion of incompetency against Davies and the way he handled the sentencing aspects of my trial. Larry wants the appellate court to have a first shot at my appeal. It all sounds like more time I may have to spend in prison, but I'll go along with whatever Marshall suggests. At least an impartial and influential person is finally examining my case, which is the number one priority.

Larry also said he's going to put some students on my case. This should be a good one for them. I'm still reeling to know he's helping me. It's the difference between night and day compared to Davies. Instead of secretive and non-illuminating, Larry is very thorough and clear. That really stretches my patience sometimes. I want to jump into the heart of things, but he starts at the beginning and takes it step-by-step. He probably reads directions before putting something together, too. Talking to him is like taking a class. I can see why he's such a good teacher.

The strain is starting to really take its toll on Ginger. Last night she was pretty hard on me. I'm starting to understand how it must be for a rape victim. *I'm* the one who was violated, yet everyone looks at me like I must have done something to cause all this. In retrospect, I could have done better, but man, *I'm* not the one who conducted an illegal interrogation, lied to the grand jury, conducted a cover-up of the investigation, and repeatedly lied under oath at the pretrial motions and the trial. I was just trying to do what I could to assist in the investigation of my parents' murders. Yes, I'm guilty of cooperating with the police. Ginger has now put my whole life on trial.

How do you figure things will go against McHenry County if Cowlin just passes everything on to the appellate court? They don't actually hold public employees accountable for their actions, do they? I figure Cowlin and Prossnitz will just publicly say, "I guess we made a mistake," while privately believing that they did the right thing all along but that they were overruled by the bleeding heart liberals who tie the hands of the police and leave society wide open for the exploits of hardened criminals. You know the routine.

Marshall said he's pulling out all the stops to get me off death row, but he also told Ginger that's not necessarily the way to go at this point. He doesn't know my case completely, though. I feel decisions are once again being made around me. I feel I have to go with whatever he recommends. The work Larry is doing now is pro bono—and you know that appeals to the cheapskate in me. It shows he's really sincere and dedicated, too.

———

RIGHT NOW IT LOOKS LIKE I'll be transported downstate next week. There are a lot of us here who are ready to go. I thought they might even take some or all of us today, and I don't know if they'll split us up or take us as a group. I have to admit I'm a little apprehensive. I've gotten quite settled here in the almost eighteen months I've been in McHenry County. From what people say, Joliet is a zoo. People hollering and screaming all day and most of the night. I've gotten used to having my own cell, but who knows what will happen there.

Let's get back to your first emergency letter. "Gary, be careful! Prison is full of shitheads!" Yeah, I know that. A few people here have told me that the best thing to do is to go into protective custody for the first four to six months until I get a feel for the place. Another fellow pointed out that PC is on lockdown for twenty-three hours a day. One hour for yard, plus chow. Doesn't sound like much, but it is survival. I'm told you get to request where you want to go, but there's no guarantee. Larry would rather I stay around Chicago, so I guess that means Joliet or Stateville. Where's Stateville?

———

THE COURTROOM DRAMA was pretty interesting. . . . Davies seemed floored that Larry showed up and announced he was my lawyer now. It does seem sudden, but Davies must have realized over the past year and a half that I didn't like what was happening. Cowlin didn't seem to want to get involved in the whole fight, but when he lifted the death penalty and changed my sentence to life without parole, it was almost anticlimactic. I wasn't particularly relieved when he did it, either—if I were still on death row, at least I'd have a private cell and wouldn't have to make the choice of PC or GP when I get moved. But we're at a turning point here. It's finally out of McHenry County.

Sixty of Larry's students volunteered to help me any way they could. They've already come out to the local bar, talked to people I knew, found out what people were saying about me, and generally doing the things Larry needs help with. He has lots of good ideas and is very encouraging, and is extremely thorough, too, which bugs me but reassures me at the same time. He's already come up with all sorts of things that hadn't ever been considered. He'll talk to me after I've been moved, and by then he'll be more familiar with the details.

After all we have paid and gotten almost nothing for, I'm getting the best for free.

Stateville 101

STATEVILLE PENITENTIARY

◆ OCTOBER 1994

Dear Nicki,

It was dinnertime on my last night at Joliet. One of the Latin Kings moved a big Kool-Aid jug closer to their table. It was a challenge to the black gangs, a turf thing. The next thing I knew, there were forty to sixty people lumped together, throwing gang signs and yelling, "Forks down"—a signal that a fight is going to start. Then the shotguns came out of the gun ports.

If I've ever seen any kind of pure evil it was when those guys started throwing gang signs. I'd never seen anything like it. They didn't seem like people anymore. The closest thing I can equate it to is when I'm working with bees. Every now and then, I'll get in a hurry or be tired and accidentally hit a couple. BUZZZZZ! They give off a very pronounced and agitated scent and all go BUZZZZZZZ. The whole hive is on Red Alert. Then half a dozen or so will make a beeline at my eyes.

As soon the gang signs started flying, I looked up and saw my cellie, Tank, standing right in the middle of it all. I asked him later what would have happened if they'd started fighting. He told me the guards would have shot right into the crowd, but I can't believe that. Dozens of people would have been hit! I'm thinking they would have fired warning shots and people would have dropped to the ground. But they sure didn't disperse when the alarm went off and the guns came out.

Tank should know, though. He was a regional leader of the Latin Kings. He'd been arrested for his first home invasion at thirteen, and at fifteen he shot a rival gang member in the neck and almost killed him. Tank told me he liked the fighting in Cook County Jail because it helped pass the time. He's a nice enough guy, real polite and soft-spoken most of the time, but every night I was afraid he'd get in on the evening shout fest. And the rap! Bomp shat bomp shat bomp shat shat shat shat bomp shat bomp shat shat shat shat shat bomp bomp shat bomp bomp shat . . .

Joliet had been busy for us. We had "yard" in the morning and I tried free weights for the first time. Not only do you have to lift the weight, but you have to balance it, too. I can now add wrist sprain to my sore elbows and shoulders. When it comes to muscle conditioning, I much prefer a sixteen-ounce, six-inch broadhead hoe, or curling twenty-pound tomato buckets.

In the afternoon we had "school," which was basically a job placement test. Math and English—no spelling, so I did okay. The only thing I'd forgotten was dividing fractions. Six and one-tenth divided by two-fifths equals fifteen and a quarter, right?

The old guys—the over-40 guys—also went to the hospital for an EKG. We had a very long wait. When I did get my turn on the table, the nurse said, "Just relax," so I went into a meditative mode and imagined white energy coming in through the top of my head and pouring through my heart and coming out as healing love. She retook my test twice, then asked me about drugs, particularly cocaine. She retook the test and mumbled something about the printer not working right before saying she'd have to try again another day. It was a good meditation. I wonder what sort of reading she got? She'd done a dozen people before me and hadn't had any problems. Must've pegged the ol' needle to the top of the graph. Do you detect a little ego there?

During the physicals the guards came in twice and said if we couldn't be quiet, the whole thing would be postponed for a month and no one would get transferred. Getting out of there was a big deal to everybody, but some of these guys just *can't* shut up. "Hey man! And fuck that, blah blah, blah!" Can't be quiet for thirty seconds. Have to talk at the top of their voices like five-year-olds. You can't tell them anything. I could see where these guys could be real problems all drunked-up and cracked-out. Then give them guns, too—shudder! What a world.

Remember I told you about the chow hall ceiling being riddled with bullet holes? I asked several people about it and they all insist the holes *are* from bullets, but after some examination and reflection on my part, I'm sure ninety-eight percent of the holes were made by apples being thrown through the panels. The hole size, placement, and trajectory are just all wrong to be coming from the guard station. Even where it does look like buckshot spray, I think they used rubber buckshot. Lead would have torn things up a lot worse. There are buckshot holes in the upper windows at the far end of the building, though, so I'm keeping an open mind on this.

———

THE FIRST NIGHT HERE in Stateville was bizarre, too. It is such a huge prison—and loud, oh God. Talk about the jive and banter going on. About one or two in the morning I heard a guy scream

Niiiiiiiiggggggggeeeeeerrrrrrssss!

And I figured it must be the biggest, baddest hippie redneck ever just trying to start something, because no one else could be *that* crazy. But no, it was one of the guards! And the black guys, they just picked up the cadence, and they're trying to grab the guy, and he's hitting the bars with his nightstick and they're all hollering . . . what an uproar! It was my first night in the state penal system. I thought, what rabbit hole have I fallen down here? I didn't even have a cellie yet. I was all by myself.

Before I left Joliet, Tank gave me the names of a couple of Latin Kings here, and said if I mentioned his name they'd hook me right up. I think I'll pass. It was nice of him to offer, though.

And now I'm here. Words can't describe Stateville. Imagine a prison in Batman's Gotham City and you have the idea. This place is right out of the early 1900s. If it had gaslights or candles, it could be the late 1800s. They've got me in what has to be the oldest building here, and this is an *old* prison. My window looks out at E house, by far the largest and most forbidding building here. Yet another monument to man's inhumanity to man.

I used a washcloth and shampoo and to wipe down the walls and floor. At least now I can look at a couple of surfaces and think they're halfway clean. Wanted to get the cell wiped down before my new cellie arrived. Didn't want to be seen disrespecting anybody's gang signs.

I moved here from x house yesterday. It's as ominous as it sounds. I was in John Wayne Gacy's cell, the one they had him in just before they executed him. My original cell must have been seventy-five years old—it had hand cranks to open and shut the door but they were so stiff they couldn't get it open. So they put me upstairs on the row. You had to walk right past the execution chamber to use the telephone in the observation room. The same telephone the governor would use to stop an execution.

My first cellie here was a nice fellow from Crystal Lake named Phil who just happened to be here because of—guess who—Judge Cowlin and an overzealous McHenry County prosecutor. I'm going to take it as providence that we ended up together. But I'm suspicious of everyone in here and it's *possible* he could have been a plant. That's incredibly remote, though, and I didn't tell him anything about me other than I, too, was a victim of Cowlin's Court. Anyway, Phil was due to be moved and is gone now.

I've spent the day second-guessing my decision to go into protective custody, but that's my nature. At this point it seems like the way to go. My inner voice has been telling me this since I first heard of the option last December.

Movement is almost totally restricted in PC, but it's restricted in general population, too. And I'm just not up to integrating some 400 gangbangers into my life right now. From what people have told me, the Devil's Disciples control GP. You have to pay for the "privilege" of your cell, you have to pay for the privilege of living at all, I guess. I don't know how bad it really is, but it sounds like an almost impossible situation for a "neutron." There are ex-gangbangers here and even they don't want any part of it.

Once a week for an hour, they open all the cells on this wing and everyone tries to use the phone. That's about twenty-five people in one hour. There are just as many showers (one) as there are phones, and everybody gets to use the shower every other day.

This is just "intro" PC, too. We'll get moved upstairs sometime. Some people say it takes about a month, but I don't think anyone down in the cells has any real idea. I still need to convince the board I need to be in PC, but I shouldn't have any problem with that, especially after an incident this morning when we went to get our stuff from Joliet. I won't get into it—it's probably nothing—but it just reminded me of the seriousness of why I'm in here and how I have to be very careful. I think I can also use the argument that my parents' murders made the news among the motorcycle people, and some bike gang member might be out for revenge against me.

The rule book says education and jobs are open to PC people the same as GP people. I sent a request letter to the education administrator today. Classes start Monday, but it's worth a try. I didn't see much on the curriculum, but I may get an interview out of the deal.

A job seems more feasible, short term. By that I mean the next four or five months. They have extensive flower gardens around here and really need my input. The ground suffers from clay compaction and is *crying* for leaves. It really shows in the plants, too. Stunted, yellowing stems in what should be such rich soil. I could really fix 'em up, but I doubt if I can get the security clearance. I'm Code Red. High escape risk. Don't give me a shovel, that's for sure! I'd be like the cartoon dog that keeps trying to dig out of jail and always ends up tunneling into the warden's office.

Damn! We're supposed to put our mail on the hatch in our door after lunch, and I just heard a noise . . . somebody knocked the letters off the hatch and onto the floor with a carton line, which is a milk carton tied to a strip of bedsheet. It looked like he was pulling the letters into his cell. They said they were just passing a TV hookup, and did in fact have one to pass, but I'm on the *other side* of the hall. There's just no supervision here. I can never be sure if my mail gets out. This time I had my own shoe line ready and didn't have any trouble retrieving the stuff, but I want this mail to go out by tomorrow. I don't know what to do with it now. There's almost never a guard down here, and when you try to hand one some mail, he just says, "It's not my job. Leave it on the hatch."

I guess I'll have to tie the stuff out there and watch for the guard. Stuff like that *pisses me off!* Some of these people just have no regard for other people at all. You should have gotten four letters so far. Three from Joliet and one from here. Did you?

————

THERE WAS A GOOD LUNCH TODAY. Beans, tortillas, guacamole, spiced burger meat, tomato, lettuce, onion, and a

BIG!

RAW!

HOT PEPPER!

Be still my foolish heart! And a great big raw jalapeño! My cellie gave me his, too. Haven't had one of those in two years. Not since the last one I plucked off the vine. Just thinking about it, I had to take a bite off the one I saved. Yep! It's real. I'm not dreaming. Hot-hot-hot heaven.

I'm on page two of your rundown of the behind-the-scenes courtroom drama with Davies and Larry Marshall. Man, this stuff is priceless. If it had been up to Ginger, I never would have heard about it. She's just too modest. Can you imagine someone having an inside track like this on the O.J. Simpson case? Oh, man, I'm getting Simpson mania like everyone else. There are scores of Simpson cases happening every day. There are about 100 murders each day in this country, did you know that?

I still can't figure Gregg's angle on this. He acts like he really doesn't want me acquitted. It's too bad Davies was so hard on Ginger, but I'm glad she saw it so she can appreciate a little more what I was going through with him this last year.

Ginger keeps feeling this pressure to sell the farm and finish this business up with Ronda, but I really think everyone should just "chill" until I can put my two cents worth into this. I mean, I *am* a part of it. There are some long-running family dynamics that need to be confronted, and hopefully, healed. We can do better than another generation of Garys and Greggs. This has all been hard on Ginger. She's really borne the brunt of it.

I've had some hard choices, and unfortunately took what appeared to be the most logical and reasonable path and "went with the flow," even though it was against my better judgment. My better judgment has really been taking a beating the last year and a half and I'm just now starting to gain confidence again in my own ability to make decisions. GP versus PC was a tough one, and it really shouldn't have been.

———

I WAS GOING TO TRY to get some paper from B.J. across the hall so I could finish this letter, using a couple of cigarettes Phil left me to use as money. He says it could be four weeks or longer for my commissary dollars to catch up to me. Then I found out B.J. is locked down, so I'll finish this letter on paper towels. Not bad, huh? I just want to get my new address here at Stateville to you. I miss your letters. I miss the news. I miss a lot.

I did get to call Ginger last night. She says Larry Marshall is coming down to see me, mostly to give me moral support. Nicki, the guy is genuinely concerned. I'm not used to that. I'm not used to having strangers show so much concern for someone they don't know, when it's not even their problem. You started it last January when you first wrote me. This is a whole new way of living for me. I've always tried to help people if we crossed paths and I thought I could be of assistance, but to go out of your way like this, well, it really increases my faith in what people can do.

After talking to Phil, I began to really see that innocent people lose their appeals all the time. He chalks it up to ineffective counsel. He says now that he's been through it and researched it himself, he probably could win if he could do it over.

I'm more and more overwhelmed that we've got Larry Marshall in my camp. Looking back, it's taken a tremendous string of coincidences to get him involved. I'm just beginning to understand how difficult it is to win an appeal. It's just incredible how people's lives hang in the balance of chance and issues they don't understand. So much of this could have been prevented.

Marshall keeps telling me this a good time to start praying.

What do you think? Should they have a mandatory civics class in high school to teach people what to do if they're arrested? How to avoid false imprisonment? They could have another class on handling your first appeal. *Miranda* rights are just the beginning. Don't get me wrong—there are some real bad guys out there. I've run into some straight-up thieves, crooks, and killers, but they know what they're doing. It's the marginal fuck-ups that are getting caught and hammered.

WE'RE STILL ON LOCKDOWN. Time goes so slowly. Until the gang leaders decide they're tired of it, lockdown will probably continue. Could just be senseless violence (like there's meaningful violence?), too. Let's see. Nothing to read. Food's still bad. No yard. No phone. No library. No commissary. That's it for news.

No, wait—there is something new. I've started making cheese! Neither my cellie nor I drink milk, and I've been saving it. I had over a gallon saved up when I processed my first batch. I got a nice four-ounce brick out of the first half gallon I tried. It looks good so far, but I won't know for sure until I let it age for a while. I don't like young cheese any more than I like milk. It tasted better than I expected, though—almost a Muenster already. There's a slight odor in here today, but once I get my cheese press working correctly that should be gone. I wonder what they'll say when we get our first shakedown. It's not against the rules (I checked) so I hope they'll let it slide. My cellie said, "Next thing you'll do is dig up the floor and put a garden in by the sink." Actually I do want a garden in here. All I'd need is to be allowed to have alfalfa seed and raw sunflower kernels sent in, and I could grow sprouts in milk cartons near the window.

I wish we had a newspaper or just something to do. This must be part of the "punishment" phase of prison. Make it a little better, then take it away and make it a little worse. Meals, too. I'm wondering if that one great Mexican lunch they served us had any significance. Onion, lettuce, tomato, guacamole, hot pepper, beans, rice, tortillas, and spiced burger meat—when the average meal is some sort of burger, two slices of bread, no condiments, one spoon of applesauce, three or four little pieces of vegetable, and sometimes a bit of ice cream. Some sort of long-range conditioning would be my guess. One guy gets knifed and everybody gets bread and water for a week.

Oh! And the showers. Have I bitched about those yet? Haven't had a warm (not asking for hot, just warm) shower since I left McHenry County. Maybe we'll get one upstairs. Maybe they're just making it really shitty here so we'll appreciate any improvements we get when we move up. "Hey boy! Remember orientation? We could put you in segregation, have to reclassify you, and start all over." I still have one cigarette. I think about smoking it sometimes, just for something different to do.

Tank had told me that if I met "Little Man" in here, he'd hook me up. Well, we have a "Little Man" just down the hall who I suspect is the bloke—in fact, that's him banging now. "Hey! Control! Bang! Bang! Bang! Control! Argue, argue, argue! @#%#$@$%!" When he came in he had a shaved head with a Confederate flag tattooed on the side. *Sieg Heil* tattoed in large red and black letters on his back. That may have been "cute" at a KKK rally in Birmingham, Alabama, but he's in Vice Lord territory now.

My cellie set his blanket on fire! It made quite a blaze. They should have let it burn out, but they scattered it and just made more smoke and ash. He had been complaining about not getting commissary. Then he flooded our floor! I got everything up on the counter in time and ended up mopping up the mess with a washcloth. He's gone now, so I'm back in cellie limbo-land. Remember the old "Mystery Date" show? Will my new cellie be a dream? Or a dud? I do like it better in here alone. When I have a cellie I feel like I'm doing *both* of our times.

You think you'll visit before Thanksgiving? Hopefully that will give me time for a shower and a change of clothes. You'll find the jail furniture is a lot less formal than the brochure implies. The chairs are scarce and in poor repair. Larry sat down in one, the back broke off, and he almost fell over backward. I told him a friend of mine collected $35,000 after a chair collapsed under her in a hospital, and Larry said, "Really! Do you know any good lawyers?"

They opened the doors for dayroom today and I felt like I was in the Twilight Zone. Everyone else was in their state clothes, blue jeans and t-shirts all around. Here I was in the yellow jumper I got in Joliet sixteen days ago. I got some strange looks and wrinkled noses as I walked down the hall.

Wonder of wonders, my counselor was in the guard hole fielding complaints so I could put my bid in for clothes. They have a little window just big enough for a lunch tray to pass through. The guards stand as far from the window as possible with their backs turned while the inmates try to get their attention by hollering their problems repeatedly. It seems that the further you can stick your face through the slot, the better the results. It's a little like what people do through the slots in their cells, but the difference is that at least one guard always has to be in the hole, so you've got someone to yell at and you don't have to get down on your knees and yell up. A few guys have mastered the trick of folding back their ears, tilting their head just right so they can stick their whole head through the slot. If I could do that, I would have clothes by now!

The counselor also explained the finer workings of commissary. The money made it into the computer, but the note I got wasn't updated yet. So it will be another week at least without coffee and hot sauce. I'm down to my last three sheets of paper, too. I've already got a couple of commissary orders floating through the system. Watch everything hit at once—I'll get two TVs, two watches, two reading lamps, and a double order of everything else—which will make half of it contraband because I'll have too many of each item.

As I was writing this, a woman in a nurse's outfit walked by handing out oyster crackers with a doctor-looking guy in tow. I expected them to be followed by a gurney and the Red Cross blood drive people. I wonder what that was all about? Why would two health practitioners be passing out crackers after supper? I'm almost afraid to eat them!

Just as I was in the middle of washing out all my cheese curds the guard came down the hall with my new cellie. An old guy. He got twenty years—I didn't even ask why. Anyway, I didn't even break stride, just flopped my sock over in the sink and in they came. The guy has a bad heart so I had to move to the top bunk. He's okay. I don't know what they'd say to me if they saw me pouring that much curdled milk into a sock, and I'm glad I got those curds washed. That's a gallon and a half I won't have to carry when they move me upstairs.

————

WELL, I'VE LANDED. Packed up my stuff and moved to my permanent home. Man! The emotions! Just knowing I'm going to be somewhere for a while. My cellie seems cool. Fixed me up with coffee right away. I'm trying not to come across as too weird. I'm sure this is stressful for him, too. Anyway, I thought I'd start crying about half a dozen times. The feelings are just starting to come out. But emotional lightweight that I am, I had three strong cups of coffee and they calmed me right down, even though I'm speeding my ass off!

My cellie *snores*. I mean he SNORES—even when he's awake. And he likes Ricki Lake! Why would anyone want to watch TV to watch a bunch of dysfunctionals fight? The guy is obviously a TV freak. Has two going on different stations at once. That is going to take some getting used to.

Otherwise, he seems fine. He's generous and trying to make me feel welcome. I'm going to try to put up a blanket as a curtain between me and the TV, and if I put toilet paper in my ears that takes some of the intensity off the noise.

We have a corner room with a view of the front gate and most of the other buildings, so that should provide some diversion. So far it's quieter over here, but "they" don't usually come out until night. I've already adapted to the top bunk, too. In a room this close at least I've got the whole top four feet near the ceiling to myself. I get the "loft" and he has the ground floor.

Our cell is right next to the shower. The cockroaches that are everywhere in this building need water every day, and the shower is the logical place for them to congregate. Sometimes they get lost and wander into our cell instead.

I had the bright idea of building bookshelves out of cardboard in my top bunk so I won't have to climb up and down to get a book. The other guys on our floor told me not to do it when they saw me hauling cardboard out of the Dumpster, because the roaches eat the paper and the glue—which provides fuel for even more cockroaches.

When you see one roach, you know there are a lot more. So when we start seeing roaches in our cell, I'll move the bookshelves down to the middle of our floor. I take the books out of the boxes and shake them as we stand, armed, waiting to attack whatever came out. Sometimes we'll have a nest of eight to ten roaches and we try to stomp on them before they run under the bed. Then we do the next box.

If we do that a few times, we don't have any more roaches for awhile. But eventually they'll be back, as bad or worse than ever. A new plan was in order.

I ordered three-quarter-inch masking tape and put it all around the doors with the sticky part partly exposed. The first night we caught sixty-seven of the bugs on the tape. My cellie got so freaked out when he saw all the roaches hanging from the tape, he decided to light the strips on fire. It was horrible. Smoking sticky strips of live flaming cockroaches.

But I did learn something about cockroach psychology. If something is happening but they can't see what it is, a roach will freeze for about a second. So I started collecting the rubber bands that came on my daily newspapers, amassing an arsenal for my next plan of attack.

I keep the pile of rubber bands next to my pillow. Whenever I see a roach, I fire off a couple of shots really fast so he freezes, then take advantage of the next second or two to take my aim. I have to move fast or he'll be gone. I've gotten so good at it that if I'm able to get off that first shot, I have a ninety percent chance of hitting him—even if he's across the room. It's like snapping your fingers and they're gone. Of course, you have to mop the floor everyday. Blood and thoraxes and legs all over the place. The rubber band literally just blows them up.

One of my cellies woke up one night screaming when I was mounting my attack. He had no idea what was going on. Rubber bands were bouncing off the wall. He had just gotten to Stateville and was having a bad experience anyway. He finally asked me not to do that when it was dark.

––––––––

SORRY ABOUT THE CHAOTIC MESS DAVIES left you. I wonder what it takes to make a case of malpractice against an attorney. Larry should be able to help me with that once he's more familiar with the case. There are so many obvious things Davies didn't pursue properly, including the police reports stating that the offender made a singular cutting motion. Prossnitz came up with the "two" or "multiple" cutting motions because that's what the police said I told them during my "confession." This was all new stuff they added for the trial. I guess they thought they could get away with it because the police reports were unclear enough.

It's really fortunate that Pandre, Lowery, and Hendle made their initial reports of the interrogation *before* the autopsies, which showed something entirely different. I repeatedly pointed that out to Davies and Russ, wrote it all down again and again, and I just don't know why they didn't pursue it. I'm so fortunate to have Larry on my case. I really wonder what reaction his students will have once they see all this. It should amaze them.

I had copies and rough drafts of all these questions, but Davies told me during the trial that I should destroy them because he wouldn't be surprised if a guard went into my cell when I was in court and got some of the papers for the prosecution. At the time it made sense. Now I wish I had kept that stuff.

So there were some names whited-out in the police report. This has got to be hard on Ginger—not knowing who to suspect really did this. Larry talks about Ginger hiring a private eye—but why should we have to investigate? That's a police job! I imagine private eyes charge about as much as lawyers. Having to be suspicious of people you normally wouldn't give a second thought to . . . sucks, doesn't it? That's got to be harder for all of you than for me. In here it's just an academic question. You guys have to live in the middle of it. It's enough to drive you crazy—the wondering. You said it's a poison that sucks you in and colors your perception of people. That says it all, Nic!

Once the Dale thing surfaced, I jumped on it. But that's just one theory. There are three strong theories right now—four, if you include me—and they all seem so unrelated. Damn! A year and a half later and it's just starting.

◆ DECEMBER 1994

CALLED GINGER—she was busy and didn't have time to talk. She said Larry was busy, too—that he had presented the fifty-fifty offer to my kids' lawyer and she was going to present it to them. I wish Ronda hadn't really screwed things up by preventing me from talking to my children since my arrest.

I went to the dentist yesterday, and right away they started pointing to teeth they want to pull. Pull! I haven't had any trouble with any of my teeth in twenty years or more, and they're talking extraction. I guess that's the only method of treatment here. I've got a cavity in one of my lower teeth that's gotten a little bigger over the years, but I have to really have to work at it to make it even slightly sensitive. So I'm going back for x-rays and they are going to discuss "strategy" with me.

I should think with a little work the whole mouthful should last me a lifetime. Phil told me a horror story he experienced when he *didn't* get a tooth pulled in jail. It eventually abscessed, and because there was no dentist there that week, he ended up pulling it himself.

People said the food would be better here than in Joliet, but it's not. Not even close. I was actually getting healthy at Joliet. Here the food is just a step above what we got at county. Damn! Bread, noodles, and grease for dinner. I ate it anyway. Now my sinuses are swelling. My ears are ringing. My brain is slowing and bogging-down. But it's too cold in here *not* to eat the food. I don't have a jacket or a t-shirt yet, but at least I got a second blanket when Phil left. Woe is me. Snivel, snivel, whimper, whine.

The guys across the hall have a little kitty. That's pretty cool. I saw a few cats running around at Joliet, too. It would be nice to have a cat if you had to do a long time, and from what I under-stand, almost everyone here got at least twenty years. I suppose that's why I met so few people in Woodstock who had ever been in a max joint. They never get out.

I wonder if Larry's crew has started anything yet. When I talked to Larry in November it seemed like this would all be in the papers by now. Now I wonder if it will ever come up. What if I am the only one who can see it? Hell, even Phil Prossnitz figured it out. He supposedly said, "To believe the defense's theory on this case you'd have to believe that police officers conspired to lie about the nature of the confession." There it is. Even he points it out. Come on, Larry. It's up to you. Man! I get tired of waiting! Where is the justice?

Why does God want me in here? Does what happen to us real-ly matter? What am I doing wrong? It's not that it's terrible in here, it's just such a waste. Whenever I start seeing a light at the end of the tunnel, I get impatient. I'd be going nuts if it weren't for Larry.

––––––––

WELCOME TO THE THIRD WORLD, GARY. My cellie seemed fine. Agreeable, friendly. Well, we got commissary yesterday for the first time. I'd been down on Floor One in a secure cell and it seemed like an opportunity to stock up. I didn't have anything I needed, like a coffee heater, mug, watch, nightlight, things like that. It came to seventy dollars for a couple of small bags of stuff.

I'd been warned about theft up here, so I stashed everything in different places so if we were hit the damage would be minimal. Well, my cellie stayed in the last couple of days instead of going to chow, so right away my antennae were up. I'd given him some stuff, but by tonight things were looking short so I pulled everything out, brought out my sales slip, and confronted him. About eight dollars' worth of stuff gone. He denied it, which surprised me. People like him just don't think about the repercussions of their actions. In this case it means I won't be able to buy any more stuff from commissary and when this supply is gone, it's gone.

I handled it like I would if I caught one of my kids taking something from me. It seemed like the appropriate approach. I calmed down right away. Fortunately, I remembered I am a child of God and this has a reason. Even as I write this it's becoming clear that responding with love is the appropriate response. I'm learning as I go. I mean, I *am* in a maximum security prison. What did I expect?

The deeper issue I need to confront here is my coffee addiction. I haven't slept for the last three nights and probably won't be able to sleep tonight, either. My overall mental state has deteriorated over the last four weeks, which just raises my suspicion level overall and constantly reminds me where I am.

. . . Nicki, it's the next day. So much for confronting your cellie and treating him like a teenager. I came back from lunch and *all* my commissary was gone! When my cellie came back he tried to run another story, but I ended up telling the property sergeant. Everything is apparently resolved now. I guess my cellie got behind on a loan or something. He apologized, which is nice.

Whew! I was reading Ron L. Hubbard's *Dianetics*—not that I'm giving any credence to his book, I think it's all a bunch of fabricated bullshit—but I was reading a part about dianetics and emotions, and he used an analogy using a toy balloon. Well, it brought back an incident when Ginger and I were very young and we'd gotten balloons from a clown at the grocery store in Richmond. When we got home the wind was strong and we both lost our balloons as soon as we got out of the car. Now I don't know why, but that incident was extremely upsetting to both of us, and we wouldn't stop crying. Ends up mom went back to Grant's and bought us a couple more balloons. That's always been an early vivid memory of my mom, and the image of the balloon in the book brought it back. But with the memory came back a remembrance of what's happened—that my mom has in fact been killed! Whew! Emotions started leaking through like water breaking a wall of sand. Man, I was almost overcome. On the one hand I'm glad to know I still have emotions this close to the surface (I've repressed them a long time) but this is no place to go to pieces.

Got rid of my cellie. The guy could be a real asshole, but he did teach me a little about prisoner manipulation and remind me that some of these guys will lie, cheat, and steal for anything, even just to stay in practice.

It also reminded me of where I am in Christ and what my thoughts and actions really should be. It is better to respond to assaults of the world with forgiveness and love. Granted this just involved some cookies and peanut butter, plus some other stuff he ripped off. I'd say in terms of value it was a sixty dollar (maybe a little more) lesson spread out over two months. Mostly it was just aggravating listening to him lie, even when I directly confronted him with the facts.

———————

IT'S EXCITING KNOWING LARRY is getting the whole picture of who I am and what the case is about. When I see him, usually he needs to gather information or discuss strategy, so I don't get much of the day-by-day drama of his work. I can imagine it happening but it's much more real and gives me a better mental picture when I hear it from you. I was hoping to get a page-by-page account firsthand when my story hits the *Tribune*. But it's starting to look like that's a luxury I'm just not going to enjoy.

There's got to be a judge somewhere who listens to the facts. But I've got to ask Larry if other people will see the truth. My own brother is familiar with the case, and if he still thinks I'm guilty, other people would too, right? I mean, he's smart. Larry gives me the impression that the appellate court judges can be just as closed-minded and conservative as the jurist I had. He said you don't hit good judges until six years into the appeal system at the federal habeas corpus level. Not the most encouraging news.

I'm still trying to get my reading light so I can stay up at night to read. That's the only time it's quiet enough to really get into a book. Then I could sleep more during the incessant daily TV. I'm trying to get back in a cell with the cellie I had before. Remember how I said his restlessness and no TV made it seem like I was doing his time and mine? I'd welcome that now. Some of the guys here just *have* to stay in a constant state of agitation. It tends to amplify an already tense situation. There are some who always seem to be right on the edge, ready to go off. Even me—some little disturbance and right away the adrenaline starts pumping.

———

I GET SO UPSET ABOUT THE TROUBLE Ginger's having with the farm—I think she's backed into a corner. Now I wonder if there will even be a farm to go back to. I trust God, but man—to give up my life's dreams? I had so many more plans than just tomatoes. I wanted to incorporate leaf recycling. I wanted to set up a pilot program to show farmers how to use them and demonstrate the results. And the farm next door: Very little research has ever been done on what it takes to reclaim chemically ravaged fields and restore them to true fertility. Especially prairie soil. People don't know which cover crops to plant, where to get seed, how long it takes, what is the most cost effective. Did I ever tell you I incorporated 9,000 bags of leaves into a 100-foot by 100-foot garden in less than two years, and got incredible results? If I have to give up and accept things, I will. But I just can't accept it being over yet.

This is my life right now. I'm trying to do *something* with it. Even being cheerful in here is challenging at times. I find myself going over a lot of negative tapes in my head, too, but they pass and I can remember that negativity isn't my normal state. Some people here are so angry and negative. Someone tore down the college sign-up sheets near the guard's station. A minor thing. But it seems like anything a little decent or positive has to be destroyed. There were once cable TV hookups in all the rooms. They're all gone. Torn out by people with no TVs, I suppose. The "If I can't watch TV, nobody watches TV" attitude. It's too bad. Well, we have an eternity to work it all out.

It's strange being the central focus of something like this yet being so powerless to affect it. This is the *slowest* roller coaster I've ever been on, that's for sure. Another six to nine months in here would probably be a realistic guess. I try to stay optimistic. I think resigned depression is worse than occasional disappointment.

◆ JANUARY 1995

I USED TO WONDER WHEN I GOT DRUNK and lost something like a wife, or tools, or a house, or whatever—what all can I lose? Shows how much I've got, I guess. Then I heard my brother wants to sell Grandpa's house now. What is his problem? Where's he coming from? I heard he, Jerry, and Ed Zender want to buy my dad's motorcycle business. What's that all about?

One recurrent memory of life on the farm was from the summer of '91, when I took my van to a back field, roasted field corn over a fire, and drank beer. Once I set up in my pepper patch by the hog shed and did the same. The memory of the fresh corn bursting in my mouth. The cold beer. Just taking an afternoon, seizing an opportunity, and really doing what I wanted to.

Building my workshop is also an especially vivid and rewarding memory. It's too bad that it only finally become fully operational the spring I was arrested and that no one will ever truly appreciate how functional it was and was still to become, with wiring, a better water heating system, and everything else. Life's cruel ironies.

◆ FEBRUARY 1995

WELL—PRAISE GOD! Things are really starting to roll. In spite of my depression and doubt. I got an express letter from Larry. It seems he has been in communication with the *Chicago Tribune* and two of their top investigative reporters have been assigned to work exclusively on my case for the next two weeks. They must have seen something. What a great thing to tell Ginger when she gets back. Two investigative reporters!

I wish now I had saved my yellow jumpsuit, the one I was so anxious to get rid of. The guard said I wouldn't need it, but at least I'd have something to wear when I get a visit. I've got some pants, but they're plastic and hot as blazes. I guess we're supposed to buy clothes, but with our current lockdown, we couldn't even if we wanted to. Other than that, I just got my I.D. rated down to blue from red. Now I'm a "medium" escape risk. Probably means I can get dental floss and shoe polish now.

I was reading a book on Mahatma Gandhi and how he would deal with crisis by fasting. It was very inspirational and inspired me to try fasting again because of what I perceive as an increasingly intolerable situation. It lasted all of twenty-four hours. A fruit and coffee fast doesn't seem like a fast track to God. There seems to be a rise in spirituality once I cut back on food, but mostly as time goes by I just feel weak and dizzy.

Life with my new cellie can be real mellow. Sometimes he gets pissed, though, which really tears up the mood. It's his style, but it seems so arbitrary to me. Manipulation. That stuff just doesn't go well with me. Someday I'll get a room where I can really get into my studies and concentrate on a book or the Bible. At least he's got some smarts, even if I don't agree with how he channels it.

Day Eight of lockdown should come off tomorrow. Someone broke into the store and stole 1,000 pounds of sugar this time, some sort of revenge for taking sugar and honey off commissary.

————

TALKED TO THE *Tribune* reporters today. It was so nice to talk to real people again! My intellect feels so limited in here. For a short time I could bask in the glow of normal human thought, resist the darker dreams and games played in here, and feel whole and real again. Deception and coercion are such limiting mental endeavors. Being as rude and evil as one can imagine is taken as a sign of success. What a culture. Is it any wonder that when these guys get out they can't live in a normal society?

I've met guys here who couldn't read or write when they got here. First they had to teach themselves to read, and then they had to teach themselves law. By going to the law library once a week, eight to twelve years into their case, they finally could seek federal relief. And that was their only recourse. Once in a while one of these guys would persevere and win an early release through his efforts. I really admire guys like that . . . talk about an uphill battle. These were guys who didn't want to get transferred to a medium prison because they had more time to work on their cases here.

When you get transferred to a medium prison, you go to school or you work. When you're in a max joint, you don't do anything. Unless you get a job as a trusty, you sit in the cage. The only time you get out of the cage is for yard or for chow—if you're not on lockdown, and we're on lockdown more than seventy percent of the time. You can submit a request to go to the law library and make copies of your legal documents, and then take them back to your cell and work your case. You can get books in, and you can get someone on the outside to work with you, and I suppose you could get copies of legal documents sent in, too.

Otherwise the guys here basically buy a TV and sit in front of it. And when the TV stays on all day, that's where their mind goes. Man, oh man! Anyone who thinks TV doesn't contribute to violence ain't paying attention. Here the guys talk to each other about stuff they saw, figuring out from what they saw on TV how they would handle real situations in their lives: who they would have to kill and who they wouldn't. The consensus is that the guys on TV didn't kill enough people and that's why they got caught. These guys are serious. That's how they think. They never would have thought of this stuff but they saw it on TV and then talked about it. Now they have a plan: Kill the witnesses and you won't get caught.

———

SOME OF MY FORMER CELLIES who weren't hooked up in gangs had tried general population, but without much success. They'd be assigned to a cell and the guy who was already there would say, "Are you hooked up?" If the new guy said no, the other guy would say, "You can't stay here." At this point the new guy has the choice of taking on the gang or heeding the warning and standing out in the hallway as soon as the cell door opens up.

The problem with this is, eventually a guard comes down and tells you to get in your cell. You can say, "I ain't going," leaving the guard with one of two options. He can call several other guards, who will knock you down and fall on you with their knees and elbows — these are big guards — to incapacitate you and cause a lot of pain before throwing you back into the cell . . . or they can write you up. Technically you're supposed to go to the hole, which is total segregation, but the hole is full of guys who carried shanks and did real crimes, so the guards quickly run out of room there and ship everybody out to PC. They had no other place to put them.

PC is filled with guys that weren't hooked up and are clueless about the whole penal system. Or they were sexual criminals — child molesters and rapists of all varieties. Others were the worst of the worst criminals. They had made so much trouble in general population that if they stayed there, they were going to get killed.

———

I'M GOING TO SEE if Ginger can try to get Nathan's address through his college in Austin. I want to write him where I can possibly get through to him without Ronda's interference. I want this all to coincide with when my case is exposed to the media. If he and Lisa learn I'm innocent, it may make this estate stuff a lot easier to work out. If you think you can help, great . . . but don't feel you have to get involved. I just wanted to write it down to get used to the idea. I mentioned it to Larry, and he said because of his involvement with my case and the way the law is, he couldn't advise me on that and certainly couldn't help me get in touch with my kids. Still, I think it's worth a try. Someday I'm going to explain what I did when I left Texas. It made sense to me, honest. How was I to know all this would happen?

I'm glad you talked to Larry. Music to my eyeballs. He's a nice guy, isn't he? Real easy to be with and talk to. I feel really "clear" around him. So clear, in fact, that I find we really don't have much to talk about sometimes. Larry talked about a "task force" and said some nice things about you. I'm glad you two are solidly connected now and that neither will hesitate to call the other should the need arise.

By the time you get this I hope exciting things about my case will be cooking in the pot. The ingredients are all there in Larry Marshall's kitchen. We've got a great chef—let's cook it up! Turn on the heat.

Love, Gary

The Appeal

Two years after my parents' murders and my arrest, Larry Marshall and his students had accomplished what McHenry County detectives and prosecutors hadn't: an effective investigation of the crime.

For a story that ran in the April 18, 1995, *Chicago Tribune*, Larry and the students took reporters on a tour of our farm, where he pointed out inconsistencies in the state's case. In the motorcycle shop, Larry described the way my parents' blood pooled on the shop and trailer floor rather than being splattered against the walls as it would have been if the evidence had matched my "confession" of slashing their throats from behind when they were standing up.

Larry hired Dr. Irving Stone, a forensics specialist from Texas, to examine the evidence. After studying the police photos and visiting the farm in March, he determined that my parents had been knocked unconscious first, and that their throats had been slashed after they fell.

But even Larry didn't know what was going on behind the scenes—that the Bureau of Alcohol, Tobacco and Firearms had identified the real murderers of my parents during an unrelated sting operation. McHenry County prosecutors knew about the discovery in September 1995, months before my appeal was heard.

It was no surprise that the federal government would want to investigate the Outlaws motorcycle gang, which was involved in a bloody regional war with the Hell's Angels that had resulted in murders, shootings, beatings, bombings, rape, and other mayhem over several years. The Outlaws funded their operations through drug deals, robberies, passing counterfeit money, and selling stolen motorcycles. They were every bit as violent as their name implied.

A local Outlaws leader, Kevin "Spike" O'Neill was a native of Twin Lakes, Wisconsin, just over the border from our farm in Richmond. By 1995, the ATF was listening to every word said in his home in Racine, Wisconsin. They planted an electronic eavesdropping device in a lamp and set up a command post nearby. The feds and the local cops listened in on and taped everything, twenty-four hours a day. The information would lead to racketeering charges—just like the ones that helped bring down certain Mafia operations.

Mark Quinn, an Outlaw who worked as an informant for the feds, knew something else. The day after my parents' murders, Randall Miller told him that they had gone to our farm to rob and murder my mom and dad. In 1995 Quinn told the federal agents what Miller had told him. By the end of the year, those agents passed on the information to McHenry County. No one from the county ever contacted me or my lawyer to tell us.

Meanwhile, Larry filed my appeal on June 8, 1995. Among his arguments:

> . . . The real proof of the emptiness of Gary's confession . . . is not simply the fact that he regurgitated the information that was fed to him, but that he regurgitated information that was later proven to be wholly inaccurate.
>
> . . . When Gary found his father, he and the others around him assumed his father had died of natural causes and that the blood they saw came from banging his head upon falling.
>
> . . . The detectives then told Gary that his parents had been the victims of foul play, and Gary started saying he could not figure out why someone would shoot his parents.

Never did he say anything about throats being cut until after the polygrapher told him that fact.

. . . With due respect to the trial judge, no evidence or testimony in this case can conceivably be construed as suggesting that "there was a mark on the decedent's head showing a particular marking which is peculiar to the top" of a knife that was introduced into evidence. The undisputed testimony (from the State's own witness) was precisely to the contrary.

. . . Gary was never searching for dead bodies when his parents were missing. He was looking for live parents and trying to figure out where they had gone for the day.

. . . According to the State's theory, Gary Gauger, who the state claimed at various times might have been in an alcoholic blackout at the time of the murder, brutally murdered his parents between 8:00 and 9:00 Thursday morning, then, within the next two or so hours, cleaned himself up to remove evidence of the crime, sobered up completely, went to work calmly in his greenhouse, and spent a half-hour chatting with a customer. Then, an hour later, Gary had enough presence of mind to go help his neighbor move some pigs, as they had previously planned. Indeed, according to the State's scenario, Gary was so successful at hiding all of the evidence that ten days of police scrutiny around the farm exposed no evidence whatsoever to tie Gary to the crime—not even evidence in the drains that someone had rinsed off blood. This strained scenario might not be physically impossible (aside from the question of recovery from possible drunkenness) but its implausibility is surely more probative of any issue in this case than are the state's suppositions about Gary's reactions to his parents' absence.

. . . we ask that the court consider some of the inherent problems with the detectives' testimony, particularly that of Detective Hendle. According to her testimony, she declined to have Gary sign a statement of his confession because the interrogation had gone on for a long time and she "wasn't thrilled about writing up that many hours of conversation." She then testified that not only was *Gary* lying when he described what happened during the interrogation, but *Mr. Frankenberry* (the polygrapher) was lying when he testified that he told her that the test was inconclusive due to a flat line response associated with fatigue, and *Ginger Gauger* was lying when she testified that Det. Hendle told her that the detectives had asked Gary to speak hypothetically about the murder. At some point it seems fair to question whether it is Det. Hendle, not all of these other witnesses, who is distorting some facts. These methods that the detectives deny using are precisely those methods that the classic handbook on interrogation instructs them to use.

. . . Nothing was ever said to Gary to suggest that he was free to leave. Quite the contrary, from the very first moment that Gary was told that he must sit in the back seat of the police car, the police gave him every indication, through their words and actions, that *they* were controlling his movements; *they* would open the door to the car if they wished; *they* would give him permission to leave the car to urinate; *they* would follow him to make sure that he did not leave after urinating; *they* would drive him to the police station without giving him any opportunity to decline; and *they* would take him to an interrogation room where they would insist that he repeat his account over and over. Gary's perception that he was in their control and was not free to leave was not some unreasonable fancy.

. . . The prosecution . . . relied on four points to show probable cause: (1) Gary "was the only person that lived with the parents" and there was "no testimony that there was any forced entry to either one of the premises"; (2) Gary had not searched for his parents in the motorcycle shop or the rug trailer on Thursday or Friday morning; (3) Gary had not called his parents' friends or any hospitals to try to ascertain his parents' whereabouts on Thursday or Friday morning; and (4) Gary did not have a visible emotional reaction upon learning that his mother's body had been found.

But, Larry pointed out:

The whole world had access to Ruth and Morris as they worked in their businesses; the lack of forcible entry did not indicate that "defendant was part of a relatively small class of people who could have had the opportunity to commit the murder."

. . . Prior to being placed in the squad [car], Gary Gauger told various officers about his activities on Thursday and Friday. Gary explained how, as his concern over his parents' absence increased, he looked around the property for some sign of his parents. Specifically, he checked the barn where his mother kept her car and he found her car there. Gary also checked the motorcycle shop and it was locked. Based on his many years of living and working with his father, Gary concluded that the locked door meant no one was inside . . . In addition, Gary checked the rug trailer, where his mother worked, and, seeing the padlock on the outside of the door, concluded that no one would be inside.

In retrospect, we now know that Gary's parents' bodies were in fact within these locked buildings. But this hindsight cannot cast suspicion on Gary's decision not to explore further once he found these doors locked. Gary was not, in his wildest dreams, looking for bodies that may have been locked inside the buildings. There was nothing the least bit suspicious about his not investigating these buildings further once he found the doors locked.

Larry also pointed out that I had no reason to panic when my parents were not home all day Thursday. They were adults, not children, and the fact that I didn't begin to call their friends to check on their whereabouts was hardly suspicious behavior. He also described the twisted logic the detectives had employed to establish probable cause:

> The officers knew, from interviewing Ed Zender and Traci Fozkos, that Gary had reacted quite emotionally to the discovery of his father's body. The prosecutor seemed to believe this was acceptable reaction for a son discovering his dead father; thus the prosecutor did not argue that Gary's reaction to finding his father's body contributed to probable cause to conclude he killed his parents. On the other hand, the prosecutor said "When the body of his mother is discovered, there is no emotion." The prosecutor argued that Gary's supposed non-emotion at that time showed that "he knew the body would be found there," and, therefore, created probable cause that he had killed his parents.
>
> Once it is recognized that Gary Gauger was unconstitutionally detained without probable cause, it becomes clear that the incriminating statements he is alleged to have

made during the eighteen-hour interrogation must be sup-
pressed.

. . . In sum, this is not a case in which the guilty will go
free because the constables blundered; it is a case in which
the constables' blundering disregard for an innocent man's
rights contributed to his wrongful conviction.

Larry argued that the State's failure to disclose information
regarding the booking officer's "blackout statement" ahead of time,
and the judge's refusal to give me the opportunity to respond,
required reversal.

The prejudice that the defense suffered from this discovery
violation is manifest and entitles Gary Gauger to a new
trial. The State countered by arguing that the defense could
have pursued the subject while Gary Gauger was still on
the stand, because the State had asked him about the statement in cross-examination. The trial court denied the
defense's request to recall Gary Gauger on surrebuttal, stating, "The question is entirely at the discretion of the court
all the way through. I think this whole thing should stop
right now."

There is no ambiguity about the State's obligation to
disclose "any written or recorded statements and the sub-
stance of any oral statement" made by the accused, as well
as a "list of witnesses to the making and acknowledgment
of such statements." . . . According to the Illinois Supreme
Court, "Compliance with the rule is mandatory and
requires the state to disclose all statements known to it,
even if the statements were not actually reduced to writing." It is a black-letter-law that this obligation applies
regardless of the state's intent or lack of intent to use a
statement during trial.

Larry wrote that the State's surprise evidence about my "black-out statement" to the booking officer was the lone piece of evidence offered to show that I ever said I had a blackout.

This evidence may well have been the key piece of evidence that convinced some or all members of the jury that Gary had not been speaking "hypothetically" during the interrogation.

. . . Had the defense been apprised of this statement in a timely fashion, Gary could have had the opportunity to explain to the jury that he became convinced that he must have had a blackout because that was the only possible way of reconciling two otherwise inconsistent facts. On the one hand, Gary had been convinced by the detectives (whom he trusted and assumed to be telling the truth) that there was absolutely no doubt that he committed the murders. On the other hand, Gary was as certain as any human could be that he had nothing to do with the crime.

. . . the State unfairly created the element of surprise by not disclosing the statement, then took advantage of Gary's surprise by arguing that Gary's uncertainty about making this statement was indicative of Gary's untruthfulness. Of course, unbeknownst to the jury, Gary's confusion was caused solely by the State's own discovery breach.

. . . Once the prosecution offered this surprise testimony in its rebuttal case, the defense virtually begged the trial judge for the opportunity to minimize the prejudice of this discovery violation by putting Gary on the stand for a short surrebuttal.

. . . Remarkably, the trial judge denied the request for a short rebuttal by stating that "I think this whole thing should stop right now," in apparent reference to the length of the trial. The fact is that the defense case had taken just one day to present its case, as compared to the eight days which the prosecution had taken to present its case.

Another major argument in Larry's appeal was that the trial court committed reversible error when it allowed the State to present testimony that I "did not pass" the polygraph examination, but did not allow my lawyers to present testimony that the test was completely inconclusive. The judge never let Frankenberry tell the jury that the test was inconclusive and that a non-result is often associated with fatigue.

The effect of the trial judge's decision in this case was to allow the jury to hear that Gary did not pass the polygraph, without ever allowing the jury to hear that the test was inconclusive. Ironically, the judge made these rulings in an effort to comply with the Illinois Supreme Court's decision in *People v. Melock*. Unfortunately the trial judge became confused about the most basic elements of what *Melock* demands and made rulings that contravened the *Melock* decision and violated the defendant's constitutional right to present his defense. . . . Had *Melock* been applied accurately in Gary Gauger's case, the defense would have been afforded the right to make sure that the jury understood that the polygraph was inconclusive. Indeed, the trial judge would have taken upon himself to be certain that there was no possible confusion on this vital and delicate matter. That . . . is the whole basis of the *Melock* decision. Yet the opposite happened.

. . . To judges and lawyers who have read about polygraph exams and understand the basics of how polygraph works, it might seem obvious that a "flat line response" or the fact that "no response could be read" means that the test was inconclusive and has no probative value. To a jury, however, these phrases could seem entirely compatible that in fact there was a result: Gary had not passed and had been detected as a liar. As the Illinois Supreme Court has explained, it is naive to assume that jurors will accurately understand what these phrases mean.

. . . Quite aside from the distorted nature of the information that the jury received about the polygraph, this conviction must be reversed because the State should not have been allowed to put on any polygraph evidence during its case-in-chief in the first place. In *Melock*, the Supreme Court explicitly limited its decision to allowing the defense to introduce such evidence, and expressed deep reservations about allowing the State to introduce polygraph evidence first.

Then, Larry wrote, the prosecutor's reference to my failure to insist on my innocence on Saturday morning when I was being brought down to the booking officer constituted reversible error. The prosecutor said it proved my guilt when I didn't protest when I realized I was being booked for murder. Yet all I was doing was waiting—finally—to talk to a lawyer before making any more statements, which was within my rights.

Miranda warnings contain an implicit assurance that silence will carry no penalty and it is fundamentally unfair and a deprivation of due process to allow the arrested person's silence to be used to impeach an explanation subsequently offered at trial.

Finally, Larry argued that the prosecutor had also distorted scientific evidence during his closing argument. Despite Dr. Blum's testimony that it was impossible to say whether the murder weapon was a knife, a rock, a hammer, or some other instrument, the State's

Attorney told the jury that the two knives police found in my greenhouse fit the "signature wound" on my mom's skull "like a key in a lock."

> . . . This argument was apparently quite powerful: The trial judge later decided to uphold the jury's verdict based, in large part, on his misimpression (no doubt created by this argument) that there "was a mark on the top of the deceased's head, decedent's head, showing a particular, as I recall, a particular marking which is peculiar to the top of the knife" introduced into evidence. There is every reason to believe that if the judge could be so misled, the jury was similarly misled by the argument which purported to characterize the expert witness's testimony.

THE 2ND DISTRICT ILLINOIS APPELLATE COURT in Elgin finally heard my case on February 6, 1996. Larry arrived with a cart full of boxes and papers. David Bernhard, the Illinois appellate prosecutor, came in with a legal pad. It was obvious Larry was the heavy hitter. And his arguments were right on. From the *Chicago Tribune* the next day:

> "The unsigned confession came when Gary parroted back what police told him during 18 hours of questioning, and his description of the knife wounds is woefully inaccurate," said Marshall (to the three appellate judges). "There is no signed confession, no eyewitnesses and no physical or scientific evidence. There was no motive. Police confiscated 163 items from the farm over a two-week period and they couldn't find any blood on knives or faucets, even though Gary is accused of washing his hands after the murders.

What this case boils down to is that Gary was convicted on the basis of the detectives' interpretation of what Gary told them when he was being questioned. The jury also was improperly told that Gary had flunked a polygraph examination.

Bernhard replied:

Counsel must have been studying a different case than I was. He confessed to the detectives and later to an inmate of the McHenry County Jail. When he called a 911 operator, he told her his parents had been dead for about a day. He showed no emotion when his mother's body was found and admitted that he didn't get along with his father. He said he resented his father from the time he was 18 months old and that Thursday was the 'best day of my life' because I didn't have to put up with my father.'

Gary admitted that his parents had been missing for more than a day and yet he goes to work in the greenhouse. He never goes to the rug trailer or cycle shop to look for them. They always left notes when they went somewhere and there were none this time.

Yet he claims it never occurred to him that they might be found in these areas, even after they had been missing for two days. This story is more incredible when this court considers that the defendant never went near the rug trailer even after he found his father dead in the motorcycle shop.

It defies belief that anyone who had lived with his parents for years and worked on the same farm as they did every day would not immediately go to the two most logical places they would be found. The defendant's contention that he did not enter those areas because the doors were locked is more than merely suspicious. It is an outright lie.

In other words, more of the same. They had their story and were sticking with it. Even though they already knew about the ATF's Outlaws investigation.

CHAPTER

14

Illegal Fruit

WHEN I HEARD I HAD A VISITOR I had a feeling it might be good news. When I saw Larry I was sure. I would have been very, very disappointed if the appellate court hadn't at least given me a new trial. And then they shot down the "confession," which made things a lot easier for everyone involved.

> . . . The record contains numerous situations that would cause a reasonable man, innocent of any crime, to consider himself under arrest. Defendant was immediately frisked and placed in the back seat of a squad car after his mother's body was found. The back seat of the squad car was sealed off from the front seat by a cage, and there were no handles to open the back seat's doors from inside. It is undisputed that a deputy sheriff was guarding the car at all times, and defendant asked permission to urinate, which he did, accompanied by a deputy. These factors clearly demonstrate that, after his mother's body had been found, defendant was not free to leave nor did he feel free to leave. The State's argument that frisking defendant was "standard procedure" is belied by Sergeant Hunt's admission that it was not a usual procedure to frisk a person in these circumstances. Moreover, the State unpersuasively asserts that defendant was kept under watch so that he could be available for questioning. There is no evidence that anyone from the sheriff's department asked defendant any questions while he was in the back seat.

Next, defendant was, in effect, told that he was going to the sheriff's department. The State's attempt to characterize this as a situation in which defendant voluntarily agreed to be driven is not borne out by the record. There is no indication that defendant was asked whether he was willing to go to Woodstock for questioning.

After arriving at the sheriff's department, defendant was read his *Miranda* rights, a factor that a number of courts have found to be indicative of whether a subject is under arrest. What followed was a prolonged and sometimes confrontational interrogation that continued uninterrupted throughout the night and into the next morning.

There is no doubt from the record that defendant was the sole focus of the officers' investigation. Moreover, throughout the questioning at the sheriff's department, he was confronted with discrepancies in his statements. Further, it is significant that not once during this long interrogation was defendant ever told he could leave. Also, defendant's testimony demonstrates that he did not feel he was free to leave during the questioning.

The State argues, *inter alia*, that because the defendant was not fingerprinted, handcuffed or booked demonstrates that he was not in custody. As noted above, the fact that these indicia of formal arrest did not occur is not dispositive.

Based on the totality of these circumstances, we conclude that the reasonable person innocent of a crime would have considered himself under arrest from the time defendant was placed in the squad car.

. . . The State argues that, even if defendant was in custody at the time of the incriminating statements, the officers had probable cause to arrest defendant soon after his mother's body was found. In support of its argument, the State contends, *inter alia*, that the above-cited statement made by defendant to the 911 operator after his father's body had been found was incriminating; that defendant did not display the proper emotions after his parents' bodies were found; and that defendant did not make the appropriate search for his parents on Thursday, April 8.

In response, defendant initially points out that the trial court never made any determination regarding probable cause. Defendant then argues that the State's contentions consist of nothing more than the argument that the officers had a hunch that something was "odd" about him and that he had reacted to his parents' death in an unusual manner.

. . . If we do not find that there was probable cause to arrest defendant prior to his incriminating statements, the arrest was illegal.

First, we note that there is no evidence that the subject officers had any knowledge of what defendant specifically said to the 911 operator. In this case, the knowledge of the 911 operator cannot be imputed to the officers at the scene of the crime. As to defendant's demeanor, the State ignores the testimony of Ed Zender and Traci Fozkos, who were with defendant when Morris' body was discovered. Both stated that defendant was very distraught after he realized that his father was dead. Further, both Zender and Fozkos testified that defendant became very concerned about where his mother was. Moreover, people's grief takes on many different forms. Nothing in the record indicates to us that defendant's reaction to his parents' deaths was so inappropriate as to be a basis for finding probable cause.

Defendant's failure to look for his parents in a concerted manner before late in the morning of April 9 admittedly raises suspicions. Yet, under these circumstances, it is nothing more than suspicious behavior. Defendant testified that it was "not unheard of" for his parents to leave their home without telling him and that he was aware of their plans to take an overnight trip with their friend, Windy.

The testimony of Detectives Lowery and Hendle demonstrates that they did not believe there was probable cause until very late in the defendant's questioning. Detective Hendle admitted that some of defendant's actions and statements aroused her suspicions. Nevertheless, she gave the following testimony at trial:

Q. What time did [defendant] become a suspect?
A. I can't say what time.
Q. Was he free to leave at 4:15 [P.M. on Friday, April 9]?
A. He was free to leave all night until he confessed.
Q. And that was at 7 o'clock in the morning, I believe?
A. Whatever time Detective Lowery and Pandre have in the report, yes.

Additionally, Detective Lowery testified:

Q. Was the Defendant at 4:15 [P.M. on Friday, April 9] free to leave?
A. Yes—any time he would have asked to leave, we would have given [him] a ride home.
Q. Why?
A. We didn't have, in my opinion, authority to detain him in an arrest situation.

This testimony serves to underscore the fact that there was no probable cause for defendant's arrest until his incriminating statements were made in the morning of April 10. Up until that time, the detectives had their suspicions and hunches but no probable cause to arrest defendant.

The State also argues that even if this court finds that defendant had been illegally detained, such an illegal detention would not have affected the defendant's confession, as it was sufficiently attenuated to dissipate the taint of illegality. In contrast, defendant contends that the State failed to meet its burden of proving that the confession was not obtained by exploiting the illegality.

. . . The fact that defendant was given *Miranda* warnings upon arriving at the sheriff's department is not insufficient, alone, to attenuate the taint of illegality. We find that the temporal proximity between the detention and confession was present here. Approximately 17 hours had passed between defendant's detention and the confession. This is not so great an amount of time as to constitute a lack of temporal proximity. . . . Similarly, we find no evidence of intervening circumstances of any significance to break the causal connection. Certainly, the time from defendant's detention in the squad car at his family's farm until the time of his confession the next morning was one continuous process. It is noteworthy that the State does not put forward any examples of intervening circumstances. Finally, there was no particular flagrancy to the police misconduct. Nevertheless, it was purposeful in that it had all the appearance of an "expedition for evidence." Under the record before us, we find that the taint of illegality had not been sufficiently attenuated to permit the admission of defendant's confession.

For the foregoing reasons, we hold that defendant's inculpatory statements were the fruits of an illegal arrest. Accordingly, we find that the trial court erred in denying defendant's motion to suppress such statements.

Because of this determination, we must address the question of whether the evidence admitted at trial was sufficient to conclude that defendant was guilty beyond a reasonable doubt. . . . We find that there was sufficient evidence presented at trial to prove defendant guilty beyond a reasonable doubt. In so determining, we make no finding of defendant's guilt or innocence, which will be binding in the new trial. Instead, our consideration of the evidence admitted at trial will protect defendant's constitutional right against double jeopardy.

For reasons stated above, we reverse defendant's conviction and remand this cause for a new trial.

Reversed and remanded with directions.

J. Rathje
P.J. McLaren
J. Geiger
Appellate Court of Illinois
Second District

———

LARRY TOLD REPORTERS he hoped I would be free on bond once I was returned to McHenry County. Under state law, an inmate must be released from prison within twenty days of a successful appeal. But the county had other ideas. The prosecution immediately filed an affidavit of intent to seek leave to appeal, trying to get the appeals court to overturn their decision.

The Appellate Court–Second District has trivialized important evidence in arriving at its conclusion that the police did not have probable cause to arrest the defendant, effectively setting a man who brutally murdered his parents free. The court's order virtually ignores the facts which the officers had at their disposal when the defendant was placed in custody. These facts would lead a person of reasonable caution to believe that the defendant murdered his parents, remembering that the police are dealing with probabilities of everyday life, not technical considerations.

. . . When the police arrived at the Gauger farm they were presented with numerous facts which pointed to the defendant as the perpetrator. The defendant lived with his parents and knew their habits intimately. He knew that they spent most of their waking hours in the rug trailer and the motorcycle shop. Yet, he claimed it never occurred to him that they might be found in these areas even after they had been missing for two days. The story is more incredible when this court considers that the defendant never went near the rug trailer even after he found his father dead in the motorcycle shop. It defies belief that anyone who had lived with his parents for years and worked on the same farm as they did every day would not immediately go to the most logical places they would be found.

The defendant's contention that he did not enter those areas because the doors were locked is more than merely suspicious; it is an outright lie.

Despite the defendant's claim that he did not show emotion like others, this statement was forcefully rebutted by his inconsolable sobbing after he finally confessed to the murders.

———

PROSECUTORS CONTINUED TO INSIST that I was the murderer and said they were considering blocking any request from Larry to release me on bond. They also wanted the appellate court to review its decision.

And Gary Pack said he won't reopen the case. He's trying to scuttle the ruling. That's mostly just a face-saving maneuver, but they're still going to try to make it look like a killer escaped on a technicality. It seemed to me that they were just digging a deeper hole, but at the same time that settled any hope I had about a total exposé of the county's methods.

But the court said no review, so the county went to the Illinois Supreme Court. Sounds like standard legal stuff—if you're not the guy sitting in prison—but this all happened despite the fact that the feds had already told McHenry County about the Outlaws connection to the murders. Of course, not even Larry knew anything about that during this period.

According to the transcripts of the wiretap recordings that we heard much later, Schneider himself wasn't worried about the outcome of my appeal. He said no one could link him to the crime. "There's nobody knows about that. . . . There's not one bit of evidence there. I had stuff on. I kept my hair (expletive) clean . . . I had all this (expletive) . . . covered. . . . There's nothing. . . . Somebody could say, 'Hey, I saw him there,' and the cops would laugh at him, cause there's no evidence from there."

Tribune reporters came out to talk to me. I told them the thing I really wanted was to have the case reopened. I didn't kill my parents and I was grasping at straws trying to come up with leads to find the person who did. It was pretty obvious McHenry County wasn't going to do anything about it.

Dear Nicki,

I'm supposed to be happy about the appellate court's decision. I'm also supposed to forgive the people who did all this to me in the first place. God help me—I can't do that by myself.

Talked to Larry yesterday. He said that due to current "politics" and a case in New York, the time is not right to appeal for bail. He's afraid the extra scrutiny and attention will do nothing except lengthen my stay here. I don't get it. I wish we'd concentrate on exposing the bogus confession and police lies and judicial misconduct.

Why is everyone so afraid of that? Nothing will ever change if small town despots think they can do whatever they please.

It's pretty mellow in here tonight. Got a bag of oatmeal and a box of grits, and the Beatles are playing "Abbey Road" on 105.9 on the radio. Apple and pear business is good. I got to play chess tonight in the library.

I'm working on my embroidery, using the sewing needle I found a while back. It was hidden in a tiny hole in the wall. Max security guys can't buy needles in commissary, but guys in medium can. I guess one of them smuggled the needle in when he got sent here for some violation.

I unraveled my shirt, sheets, and pants to get different colors of thread. I made a tote bag to carry things around in, a pair of bell-bottoms, and even a Calvin & Hobbes patch. Some nights I start sewing around eight in the evening and before I know it, I hear the guy coming with breakfast. Just like that, the night is over. It's a good way to pass the time and I'm usually so tired I can sleep the day away.

A person really appreciates the little things in here.

––––––––

WE'RE LOCKED DOWN AGAIN. It seems that a guard got stabbed last Thursday and we've been on lockdown every since. No telling when we come off. I had started to look forward to a decent routine, a little chess, some social activity at meals—and poof! It's gone.

All my precious contraband was taken away thanks to the Orange Crush. The Orange Crush is a group of guards in goon suits who take great pleasure in crushing you if you step out of line. I assume they are guards from various prisons trained in riot control. They come into the wing like stormtroopers—STOMP STOMP STOMP—in an obvious effort to be intimidating. They look the part, too—orange suits, helmets, face shields, clubs, knee pads. Full armor. They kick you out of your cell, tear apart your room. I saw one guy challenge them and four guys came down on him with elbows and knees. He was basically crushed.

Orange Crush came in to shake down the whole prison after several guards were stabbed. There is an ongoing war between the gangs and the guards—basically, the gangs don't recognize the guards as authority figures. The Orange Crush completely searched every cell. It took months—there were 1,500 cells. Rumor had it they found a gun, cell phones, and lots of money—stuff the regular guards had brought in, no doubt.

I hid my Calvin & Hobbes patch in a book way in the back of my room, but they found it. Gone. The only contraband they didn't get was my extension cord and my razor. I had sewed it up in my mattress. I would have hidden more that way, but was afraid I wouldn't end up with the same mattress when the shake down was over and everything got put back in the cells.

They took all our fans. The electric fans they gave us are so inadequate that we cut the plastic face off to get a little more air flow from the blades. As soon as you modified the approved fan design, you were technically harboring contraband. The local guards didn't worry about it, but the Orange Crush took everything that wasn't completely regulation. We're allowed one blanket—I had accumulated five, so they took four of them. All my spare fabric, my bellbottoms, my hippie flowered tote bag—straight to the Dumpster. They didn't find my needle and I've made a few more things since, but my heart isn't in it.

I want out.

I'm getting tired of my cellie, too.

Like yesterday. It's Saturday night. He's turning the radio dial. All these great FM programs, and he picks talk radio . . . Newt Gingrich! Newt Gingrich! What an idiot! The usual fascist ravings. Saying absolutely nothing useful. Just spare the government any responsibility for poor people and leave us alone so we can stay rich.

I owe everybody letters but can't get started. Who wants to listen to this ranting? And Larry says don't try for bail? Gregg is trying to fuck the whole farm up again. Looks like we'll have to pare the farm down to forty acres and be happy if we can keep that.

Larry is supposed to come this week with an estate lawyer. I got a letter from Ginger, too. It seems Gregg is pushing for a quick sale and threatening to have Ginger removed as executor. Ginger agrees with me that preserving at least the forty-acre homestead is paramount at this point. She feels that can still be in real jeopardy. As she said, that farm is the only place either of us has really felt of as "home" and the only piece of land anywhere either of us has any real attachment to. Plus, to lose it would probably result in a total split of the rest of the family.

I've had six people mention the *Tribune*'s last article on me. It pissed me off enough to keep going through the trial abstract Larry gave me. I've been through it once—I need to hit it again to refamiliarize myself with the more obvious irregularities of the cases in here—"regularities" seems more the situation. That's one reason I feel this needs to be brought out, so this type of courtroom/police practice doesn't go unchallenged.

Phil Prossnitz was more horrible than Hendle, Lowery, and Pandre all put together, if that's possible. I don't see how they could have allowed his closing argument to continue. I'm so upset I can hardly write about it. Something's got to be done to expose this. I just don't know what to do. Larry tells me to wait until I'm out.

Plus, when Gary Pack said he wouldn't reopen the case—he felt he already had the killer—well, I just can't let this die down and be swept over. That pretty much drew the line in the sand for me.

Am I just being impatient again? Larry says "just cool it" for a while, but I'm afraid that once I'm out, if and when that happens, that'll be it—no one will care.

Home

NOBODY TOLD ME I was going to be released that day. When they fetched me from my cell in Stateville, I still didn't know anything. It wasn't until later that morning that they told me I was going to Woodstock and that I was going to be on a leg monitor at home.

When I left, I figured I was going up to Woodstock for another hearing or even a new trial. I figured I'd be back at Stateville before long—if I knew this was the end of my stay there, I would have given my cellie all my coffee. I hope he found it before they cleared out my bunk. He didn't have much money for commissary and could have used it.

Ginger and Nicki called Sue at work and told her I was probably going to be released that day. There was a group waiting for me when we got to Woodstock. They didn't fit the monitor there— it had to be calibrated with the phone at our house.

So for the short ride in Larry's car from Woodstock to the house I got to ride as a free man. A carful of Larry's students followed us. We even stopped at Ellison's in Hebron for ice cream before heading east on 173 toward the farm. We had ice cream in jail a few times, too—it came in a cup with a cover and a little wooden spoon that can't be made into a shank. The same thing they give first graders, though for different reasons, of course.

When we got to the house, none of the guys from the county were happy. The guy from the sheriff's department who fitted me with the monitor seemed rather aghast that this was all taking

Photo by Jerry Tomaselli

Gary with Larry Marshall, talking to reporters at the McHenry County Courthouse the day he was released.

place. When I asked him how far the monitor allowed me to go, he didn't even answer.

Lars picked Sue up at work and met us at the house. There was a press conference the same day. All the reporters who got wind of what was happening jumped right on it. I was still dazed . . . I don't remember too many details of that day. In fact, the next couple of weeks were a kind of blur.

It turns out I had a fifty-foot restriction, but Ginger wouldn't let me go more than twenty or thirty feet from the house. She wouldn't let me go to the tool shed that was only about forty feet away. She didn't want me to have any blots on my record or give the police any reason to come out. The very next day Ginger had to go somewhere and she asked Sue to come over and babysit me. She didn't want me to be alone the second night I was at the house. That first week was rough. I couldn't sleep. I've never become my old self, even now, so I can only imagine the shape I was in for the first several days.

Photo by Jerry Tomaselli

Ginger, Nicki Nelson, Gary, and Larry Marshall after Gary's release.

I spent my time building a porch on the house. I did an incredible job. I dug around the foundation five and a half feet below the dirt line and tuckpointed all the rocks. I had a wooden walkway over the trench where I was fixing the foundation. When a customer would walk over it to go into Ginger's shop, I'd startle them by calling out, "I'm the Billy Goat Gruff!" I did the foundation work in the back around the cellar door, too. That was all I had to do, after all.

There was no legal reason left for the county to keep me on house arrest, and on October 2, they took the leg bracelet off. I walked over to Fred and Joanne's and smoked a joint, got stoned, and walked around the woods. Ginger was adamant that I didn't smoke a joint around the house. She was afraid I'd want to get drunk and run down to one of the bars. She thought she was responsible for keeping me on the straight and narrow.

Friends tried to keep me busy in the evenings. Sue and Lars took me to dinner in Harvard. Nicki and Steve took me to a movie. She told Sue later that I was wandering around in the lobby, talk-

Nicki Nelson and Gary talk with reporters at the farm.

Photo by Jerry Tomaselli

ing to myself. People who know me well were used to that, but she knew me mainly from our letters back and forth and was worried about how I was acting. She asked Sue, "Aren't you just a little afraid of being alone with him? He just doesn't seem right."

In February 1997 I moved into the greenhouse. It was hard living with Ginger and Evan—hard for me, but it was also hard on them, having me around all the time. I think I just needed to be on my own. My bed was a piece of plywood balanced on two sawhorses, and I slept better there. Nicki brought over a camping cot, air mattress, and a blanket, so I was living in relative luxury.

Sue came out to see me on Tuesdays, her day off. She helped me out in the greenhouse—at first, just getting things fixed, then with starting seeds in the late winter. Maybe she was lonely. I know I enjoyed her company. She helped me build a cold frame sash, transplant vegetables from the greenhouse to the cold frame, move tomatoes. I taught her how to drive a tractor.

A couple of months later, as I got to know Sue better and looked forward more and more to her Tuesday visits, I realized that our relationship was changing. A little more than a year after I was released, she moved out of her own house and into the greenhouse with me.

From that night on, we lived in the greenhouse until we moved into what had been my grandparents' little white house. There were tenants there and we had to wait until they moved out.

Sue and I lived in the greenhouse with Sue's dog and two cats. It was like camping. We coped. We had an outhouse. We heated our water in the woodstove. Sue would wash her hair and rinse it outside.

————————

ONE OF THE MOST ROMANTIC THINGS I've done was getting my lawyer to make it easier to propose.

In October 1999, Larry, his wife Michelle, and their two little girls came out to the farm to get their Halloween pumpkins. They had spent the day in Lake Geneva and one of the girls, who was three years old, had refused to go to the bathroom all day.

Sue convinced her to go at our house before the long ride back to Chicago. The Marshalls said their goodbyes, and later that night Sue asked me if Larry and I had taken care of all our business during the visit. We had some legal things to discuss, and also made arrangements for me to talk to a class at Northwestern during Public Interest Law Week.

I told her yes, then added: "By the way, we're getting married November 11."

Sue said, "*What???*"

I said, "Well, I had mentioned to Larry that we were thinking of getting married so Larry got on his cell phone to Matt Kennelly, a friend of his who just became a federal judge. Larry said we'll have lunch with the judge at noon, we can get married at two, and then I can do my talk at four."

The whole arrangement appealed to the cheapskate in me. I'd save forty bucks since the judge said he'd do the ceremony for free.

Sue claims I never mentioned the wedding plans until the night after the Marshalls left. I thought I told her when she came out with little Hannah. Either way, she said yes.

Ginger gave us one and a half years. Larry's advice was: Don't fuck this up. But on November 11, everything went smoothly. People in Larry's office brought potted begonias. Nicki was a witness, but more than that, a real friend. She had supported me with her letters, and supported Sue after she broke up with Lars. Steve Miller, one of the students who had worked with Larry to free me, was there. After my talk, we all had cake and cookies.

Sue had wanted me to wear a tie, but in the excitement didn't realize until later that it had been in my pocket all day.

Larry and Michelle took us out for a very nice dinner and gave us a night in a suite—which, by the way, was as big as the entire house we lived in on the farm.

For someone who shunned lawyers my whole life I now know so many, it's incredible.

Gary and Sue on their wedding day.

Photo by Nicola Nelson

One Percenters

OCTOBER 12, 2000. Three years and four months after police and ATF agents arrested fourteen Outlaws in a morning raid, Chief U.S. District Judge J.P. Stadtmueller sentenced Randy "Madman" Miller to life in prison. The judge said he would have given the man who killed my dad the death penalty if he had the choice because Miller had participated in an "incredible series of barbaric acts we only find in Third World, uncivilized societies."

Six months later, I sat with Ginger and Gregg in the courtroom in Milwaukee when James Schneider received his sentence: forty-five years in prison. The man who had killed my mom was the only Outlaw indicted in the federal racketeering case who cooperated with prosecutors—not surprising, since the Outlaws' motto is "snitches are a dying breed." He was also the last defendant sentenced.

Before he read the sentence, the judge said my parents' murders were the most disturbing of all the crimes Schneider admitted to because everything he had heard during the trial indicated that my mom and dad were gentle people who had nothing to do with motorcycle gangs or their other "dastardly acts"—the murders, bombings, and arsons they had done in the name of the Outlaws.

"They were not rival club members. They were just honest, small-town folk trying to live out a dream in America," Judge Stadtmueller said. "You and Randall Miller snuffed out that dream."

The three of us listened as Schneider apologized. "The thing I took away from them . . . they'll never be able to smile with their parents again," he said. "I can't erase the pain . . . the pain and suffering of Mr. Gary Gauger, who I don't even know."

He asked for forgiveness, too, but said that if he were in our shoes he didn't think he could forgive. "To be truthful, your honor, if it was me this happened to, I wouldn't be able to forgive someone who stole my parents from me without a chance to say goodbye."

I believed his apology and told reporters so, although my first thought was: It's amazing how sobriety had improved his thinking. I said I was glad that Schneider had decided to cooperate with the prosecutors almost as soon as he was arrested. There were so many details in his testimony that brought some finality to what had happened that day. It was a tragic situation all the way around.

James Schneider was just thirty years old when he killed my mother. At the time of his arrest he worked as a heavy machinery operator at an excavating company in Volo, Illinois. Before that he had worked at a sports bar in Lake Geneva, just across the street from the café where he had breakfast with Randall Miller after they killed my parents. He had also worked in various factory jobs and at a body shop.

He grew up in Milwaukee and lived there until he was about 21, when his mother bought a tavern in Delavan, Wisconsin. He worked for her there for five years. That was when he got to know the Booze Runners and started to cover for them when the police were called after bar brawls.

He eventually became a probate for the Booze Runners, then for the Outlaws when the two gangs merged to be the Wisconsin Outlaws in 2000. Normally the Outlaws wouldn't have taken a whole group at once, but because of the war they were fighting with the Hell's Angels, they did. The first thing they had to do was kill the president of the Hell's Angels club in Rockford—they were serious. Schneider testified that Randy Miller took part in a bombing at a Hell's Henchmen clubhouse in Rockford. He and another Outlaw got the ss lightning bolts for this job, a status symbol.

When Schneider became became "full patch," he got the Outlaws patch, a diamond-shaped "One Percenter" patch, and an American Outlaw Association patch, which had a hand with the middle finger extended and a swastika on the back. Back in the '60s, the American Motorcycle Association had insisted that only one percent of bikers were renegades and that the rest were upstanding, law-abiding citizens, and the Outlaws took the slogan for their own.

At first the "missions" Outlaw leader Kevin O'Neill assigned to Schneider involved drug deals. As the turf war with the Hell's Angels escalated, things changed. The Mississippi River was the informal dividing line between the two clubs. The Hell's Angels were moving east into Outlaws territory and the former Booze Runners were put to work as enforcers in the war.

My dad didn't do much business with the Outlaws, although it turned out that Kevin O'Neill did have a Harley and he was at the farm couple of times. I remember seeing a couple of guys at the shop wearing Outlaws jackets—they could have been Miller and Schneider, but I really don't know. One was bigger than the other and they both had long blond hair. I noticed the jackets because they had very distinctive graphics—pistons and a skull. But my dad never said he had any trouble with them.

Schneider testified that Randy Miller told him he wanted to rob my father's motorcycle shop because he knew my parents had a lot of money on the property.

The reason that he knew this was sometime previous, maybe a couple of weeks, I'm not certain how long, Randy Miller and Harry Morgan and Steve Dunn, all Wisconsin Outlaws, had driven to the place, to this motorcycle shop, the Gaugers'. Randy Miller and Harry Morgan went into the shop. There was no one around. They found a paper bag with a thousand dollars, I believe it was, that was near a wood burning stove.

That is what got Randy Miller going, thinking that there was a lot of money there because he found this paper bag with money. It had been burned from being near the stove, so he assumed that with Mr. Gauger being old that he did not believe in banks, that he just stashed all the money from his motorcycle shop in the house or in the motorcycle shop itself.

He and Harry Morgan went back to the road. They were picked up by Steven Dunn. At that time they gave him, I believe it was ten dollars out of the thousand, and they told him, "This makes you a real One Percenter." . . . they used to joke about that.

Randy Miller . . . said he and I should go down there and we should rob the people, that we would get a lot of money out of it. They were old people. So we went down there. We went down a series of nights. We went down the first night to basically survey the house, to get a feel of what was there. . . . I picked him up at his house. We drove down to the Gaugers' in Richmond, Illinois. It was about a half-hour-long trip. We surveyed the house, kind of got a look around, decided that we would go back the next evening, hold the people at gunpoint and rob them.

All the times that we did go down there we were armed —I had a 9-millimeter semiautomatic pistol. Randy Miller did also. We also had knives with us. At this time it was just going to be a robbery. He said, "If we go in and force them at gunpoint, they'll tell us where all the money is."

We went down the following night. I picked Randy Miller up again. I drove down there. We were going to rob them, rob the people this night. We got down there and there was another vehicle in the driveway. With another vehicle there we didn't want to go in and rob them at this time.

After we left there and drove back . . . Randy Miller brought up the idea. "Well, if we kill the people then no one can identify us. They can't pick us out of a police line-up or mug shots or anything like that." So the following morning I picked Randy Miller up early in the morning, perhaps five thirty in the morning.

All the times that we went we wore gloves. We wore older clothes. I had long hair at the time, a lot longer than it is now. I had it pulled up and tucked underneath a base-ball cap. We went down there that morning. Now it's under the assumption that we're going to murder these people. Randy told me, "I want to have the people separate. I don't want to kill them both together. . . . You'll kill one person. I'll kill the other."

We pulled off on the side of the road, took the license plates off the car. This was a couple miles before we got down to the Gauger farm. Once again we were both armed with pistols and knives. We decided instead of using the guns because they would be too loud that we would use the knives to kill the people with.

Schneider continued his testimony, giving complete and graph-ic details of what he did to my mom and what he heard when Randy Miller killed my dad. Unlike the details in my so-called "confession," his description of the murders matched the forensic evidence found at the farm.

By the time Schneider was sentenced, I had already filed a civil suit in federal court for wrongful arrest and prosecution. The coun-ty fought me every step of the way, despite the information the feds got from the wiretapping and testimony like Schneider's. At first, when the feds first got wind of the wiretap confessions and told

McHenry County about them, the county prosecutors didn't take action because they said they weren't sure how reliable the admissions were and how much they could say publicly because of the ongoing investigation.

There was a big press conference at the farm when the bikers got busted on June 10, 1997. Things took off from there and there were interviews and programs on nationwide networks. Larry and I both said we were glad to hear the news, but didn't want to jump to conclusions. He told the *Kenosha News* that I knew firsthand that "just because people have been indicted, it doesn't mean they're guilty." In an article in the *Northwest Herald*, he said: "They want justice for the people who killed their parents. They don't want another set of wrongful convictions."

Phillip Prossnitz told the *Chicago Tribune* that "important information linking the slayings of Gauger's parents to Outlaws members began trickling in" while I was in prison. Larry Marshall said he was disturbed that prosecutors kept fighting my release despite the evidence that was coming in. Prossnitz was also interviewed in the June 11 *Northwest Herald*. So was my brother.

> . . . Another Gauger sibling remains unconvinced. Gregg Gauger, an older brother who lives in Whitewater, Wisconsin, said Tuesday he still believes his brother may have killed his parents or was otherwise involved.
>
> "I want to wait and see what the facts are," Gregg Gauger said, noting he planned to study the indictment today. "On the basis of the evidence presented at trial, I think the jury made the right decision," he said about his brother's trial, in which the jury found him guilty in three hours. "I also agree with (Cowlin) that there was justifiable suspicion to detain Gary for questioning."
>
> Any lingering doubt over whether he committed the two gruesome slayings appear to be dispelled now, at least in the

minds of police and federal officials involved with RICO investigation.

Thomas Schneider, federal attorney for the Eastern District of Wisconsin, said police involved in the RICO investigation knew Gary Gauger had been convicted for the crimes and took steps to keep local officials informed as they developed information.

"As soon as we became aware that there was potentially exculpable evidence, we made sure we were working with them and made the evidence available as quickly as possible," he said.

It's not clear what the exact timeline was and how long—or why—Gary Gauger remained in prison after police began to suspect motorcycle gang members. Gauger's attorney, Northwestern University law professor Larry Marshall, said he had been kept informed by local officials for the last year or so of ongoing developments.

McHenry County Assistant State's Attorney Philip Prossnitz, who prosecuted Gary Gauger, agreed with Schneider's explanation of how the case was handled. He noted he had been "in constant communication" with Marshall.

"It's been a delicate balance for everyone involved, including the ATF, the U.S. Attorney's office, the [McHenry County] State's Attorney and Professor Marshall," Prossnitz said. "It's important to remember that while we obviously wanted to fully and completely assist the ATF with their investigation, we also had an obligation to allow the jury system to complete its work."

. . . As to the new evidence, which, if accurate, appears to clear Gary Gauger at least of direct involvement in the murders, Prossnitz said he would take a wait-and-see attitude.

"As of yet, there has not been a finding of guilt on the charges," Prossnitz said. "It's important to allow the legal system to work."

Leaning against a tree Tuesday in the yard of his family home, Gauger looked like any farmer taking a late-afternoon break on a hot day. A teal Goofy baseball cap shaded his lined face, and dirt smudged his palms and caked his fingernails.

He spoke enthusiastically about farming the land again after years in a jail cell, even inviting the gaggle of reporters surrounding him to come back at harvest time for some sweet corn or squash from his vegetable stand.

. . . They [prosecutors] zeroed in immediately on him as the murderer, their case resting largely on a partially inaccurate confession Gauger said was only a hypothetical explanation of how his parents could have been killed.

"They're supposed to be on my side," Gauger said, his voice full of emotion. "I trusted them. I believed them. I relied on them. I needed them.

"And they took that trust and they dashed it."

Marshall said it was too soon to talk about lawsuits or other avenues of redress for Gauger. But he said the case is a textbook example of the criminal justice system run amok and thinks an independent investigation would be in order.

But for now, Marshall said Gauger's primary focus is helping investigators discover if they finally have found the people responsible for their parents' murder.

"I wish they would do their job," Gauger said. "Seek justice. Don't seek convictions."

In Spite of the System

I HADN'T EVEN CONSIDERED suing the county until after I was released and the ATF busted the real killers. Even though the facts of my case and the violation of my constitutional rights hadn't changed, I don't think people took my claims very seriously before the Outlaws were arrested. That all changed once the crime was actually solved.

But the county continued to fight. According to a story in the *Northwest Herald* in April 2003, McHenry County paid more than $1 million to attorney James Sotos between 1998 and the end of January 2003 to defend county prosecutors and sheriff's detectives during my civil rights lawsuit. They're still fighting and taxpayers are still footing the bill. Ironically, I'm one of those taxpayers.

People always ask me if the state gave me any kind of financial compensation once it was proved that I had nothing to do with the crimes. The answer is no: There is no automatic compensation if you are unjustly convicted of a crime. Compensation is the exception, not the rule. And to get any kind of compensation from the government, you have to be pardoned first. Not just exonerated and released, but pardoned by the governor. Right away that implies you have the governor's ear and he's convinced you are innocent. This takes money—there is a lot of legal paperwork. Larry did my work pro bono, and for people in other high-profile cases, lawyers will help them for free, too. Otherwise, there's not much chance of getting it done.

The end of 2002 was a legal roller coaster for me. I filed my application for a pardon in September. Within days, Judge Philip Reinhard dismissed my lawsuit against the prosecutors and detectives. He said although Hendle, Pandre, and Lowery had lied to me about the evidence they said they had and about the results of the polygraph, they hadn't broken the law. Police don't have to tell the truth. They have to turn over all written exculpatory evidence and they did, but they don't have to tell the prosecution about stuff that isn't written down, even if there was nothing written because they destroyed their notes.

So I couldn't sue them for what they did in court—it had to be for something they did before trial. And there was a statute of limitations on such suits—the court said that in some cases that limit didn't apply, but nevertheless I could only sue for what happened from the time I was arrested until they charged me the next morning. The police "only" damaged me for twenty hours. The prosecutor was only doing his job because the cops told him I confessed. They did a million dollars of damage to my head, but it would be difficult to prove. People would say I was crazy before. We appealed the ruling. As I write this, more than five years and many setbacks later, the final outcome is still pending.

I thought my application for a pardon would be a slam-dunk, because the crime was solved by the federal government—but the county prosecutors opposed it. They did such a good job that I'm sure they convinced the prison review board to recommend against a pardon. But Gov. George Ryan knew my case personally and pardoned me on December 19.

Compensation came a couple of years later. The standard amount used to be about $3,000 per year for the time you served, but because of a couple of other high-profile cases, the state raised it to about $10,000. My total check, including interest, came to about a third of what my first lawyers billed me for the trial.

During the deposition for my civil suit, they walked me through the night of the interrogation and I literally had a mental flashback of three in the morning when they got me to do the scenario. It took me a week to try to think again. The next day I couldn't even drive my truck around the farm. I couldn't talk. It was like I had a stroke. I couldn't form sentences to express how I was feeling, and I was very frustrated and short with people. This was six or seven years after the actual interrogation! At least I knew what was happening. For months after the deposition, during the whole summer, whenever I would go to back my truck out, I always turned so I would back into the barn instead of turning into the driveway. During the flashback, something got twisted in my brain and the things I would otherwise do automatically I would do wrong. I would always park the truck by a certain tree and was supposed to back out, go left, and pull away. But the rest of the summer I always went right and ran into the barn every time. Even if I sat there and thought about it, I would do it wrong. I had to reteach myself how to back out of that parking space. It was interesting to observe what was happening in my brain, to see how the psyche can respond to a trauma years later.

I sometimes look at myself in the third person. A lot of exonerated guys, including Anthony Porter, do this. During speaking engagements he would say things like, "Anthony Porter was put in the hole." "Anthony Porter can't see because of light deprivation in prison." It's a defense mechanism I recognize in myself. You're not talking to Anthony Porter or Gary Gauger, you're talking to the guys that look out for them.

After I spoke to one of Larry Marshall's classes at Northwestern, I figured I was done—I had told my story. But I wasn't. It took me a long time to get used to that. When people called me for interviews, my first impulse was to say no. I did say no when I was invited to go to Italy for a TV show. I had just gotten out of jail—I didn't want to go traveling around the world.

But usually, every time someone would ask me to go somewhere and tell my story, all I could do was think back to when I was in Stateville whining to Larry about the *Trib* article. No one wanted to listen, nobody cared . . . and Larry said, "You'll get your chance to speak."

And I have. I've been on *Oprah. 60 Minutes. 20/20, Connie Chung Tonight* on CNN. *NewsHour* with Jim Lehrer, Court TV, *Montel. Larry King Live, A&E Investigative Reports.* Reporters from 12 different European countries (including Germany, five times) have come to our farm to film or conduct interviews. Jessica Blank and Erik Jensen came to visit during their cross-country trip to interview me for their play, *The Exonerated*, which tells the stories of six former death row inmates in their own words.

I still get panic attacks, if that's the word, when I do speaking engagements. Sometimes these spells last a couple of days, sometimes only for a few hours. Sometimes it's not bad at all, but I can get anxious just by talking about what I went through. During a

Photo by Julie Von Bergen

Outside the 45 Bleecker Theater in New York, where the Culture Project's long-running production of The Exonerated *featured stage, screen, and music stars in the roles of six former death row inmates.*

trip to New York to play myself in *The Exonerated* in 2003 I was nervous, but it wasn't bad because I was reading a script. I was an actor, even if the words were my own. The hardest time was a three-week trip to Alaska for a speaking tour—sometimes I'd do four engagements a day. I'd hoped the experience would desensitize me but all it did was wear me out.

I wasn't sure until I did these things what the reaction would be—what the audience was getting out of it or what I was getting out of it. The stuff that happened was unexpected. It really expanded my conscious universe as I learned how things work, how other people understand things. I wasn't aware of the effect I was having on other people. Five or six years after hearing me people would come up to me and say things like, "I changed my major and I'm studying law now." Nicki started studying to be a paralegal and is now an attorney. We started getting laws passed. I found myself talking with Jesse Jackson Jr. in Washington, D.C., when he kicked off his campaign for a nationwide moratorium against the death penalty. I realized we were actually having an effect. I talked to Harvard Law School students in Cambridge, Massachusetts, about my experiences. It was incredible.

I am so impressed with the mothers of the death row inmates tortured into confessions by the notorious John Burge of the Chicago Police Department. They made me realize that injustice doesn't just happen to the guys involved—it happens to the people who care about them.

The only person who influenced me more than those women was Dennis Williams. His story is so horrendous. He was arrested when he was nineteen or twenty and spent seventeen years on death row before his case was solved by journalism students. It turns out it was a really easy case to crack. He was within two months of being executed. Just looking at the man, you could tell he had a lot of hurt. No anger, but hurt.

These stories inspire me to go out. I can't *not* do it. Especially me. I was on the fast track for rescue. By the time my feet hit Stateville, I had sixty students and a university behind me. So many other guys had a dozen years in prison before someone even started looking at their cases. That's why when people say, "See, the system worked. The real killers were arrested and you got out," I say, no, I was released *in spite of the system*. The timing was right for me. The Rolando Cruz story was huge—a complete circus. Eric Zorn of the *Chicago Tribune* did a great job exposing it and made the state look so bad.

Getting Larry and Northwestern University on my side gave me credibility. Other guys on death row may say they're innocent, but people just shrug their shoulders and say, "Everyone in prison says that. These guys are all liars anyway."

Speaking to classes is sometimes the hardest. I try to make it real, especially in an intimate setting like a high school. It's hard to get on a soapbox and separate myself like I can sometimes do in a big group. Sometimes when I'm done, I tell myself I'm not doing any more.

I don't bring notes with me to my speaking engagements. I try to find out beforehand how much time I have and what the focus should be. It depends on the group. Death penalty abolition groups are working platforms and want to get people interested in their cause. Law students focus more on the legal abuses. With high school students I focus more on the bad food, the fights, the cockroaches in Stateville, the judge making faces at my trial, the perjured testimony. Things they can relate to.

Larry is now teaching at Stanford University in Palo Alto, California. We took a trip out there in February 2005 to speak to some of his classes. The topic was aimed at law students and how lawyers handle involvement with their clients. They want to be close enough to their clients to be able to represent them, but not too involved, especially in a death penalty or any other difficult

case. It's just too hard. Larry also wanted students to think about
how much lawyers can ask their clients to do to help them with
their own causes. Where are you using them and where are you
helping educate the public? I told the students I don't feel used. I
had been whining and complaining that no one would listen.

I hadn't done much the winter of that trip and I made up my
mind that California would be fun—until the day before we left.
I started to panic a little. When I got there I went into manic
mode, which didn't surprise me. This had happened before. I got
very animated. My brain sped up. I was schmoozing, talking with
everyone. There was a modern dance interpretation of my case. We
hung out with the cast of *The Exonerated*, which was being presented that week, and talked to the audiences after the perform-
ances. I have so much I want to say and sometimes I give too much
information. I don't know how much the audience knows already
and I just want to tell them everything.

Sue says that on some of the trips she's been on with me, I'm
so bad I can't even get out of bed. Sue doesn't even remotely expect

Photo by Julie Von Bergen

Gary and Sue (center) and cast members of The Exonerated *speak
with audience members at the University of Wisconsin–Whitewater
in 2006.*

me to remember our day-to-day itinerary. It's like traveling with a ten-year-old. She makes sure I don't have anything to do when we get home beyond the usual farm routine.

Without Sue I wouldn't be able to do nearly as much. Or maybe I'm using her strength and organizational skills as a crutch so I don't have to keep myself organized.

When I got home from California, I went through two very distinct phases. I was burned out and depressed for about four days. Then I went into my normal "farm" mode. I took about a week to recover.

One of the reasons people keep asking me to do these speaking things is not that I'm all that profound. It's that I show up. A lot of other death row guys don't. They say yes when they get the call, but when the time comes they go through something like I do. They panic and think, "Fuck this shit." They get high or drunk or just disappear. They've been through it all before and I bet it has the same effect on them as it does on me. I show up because I have Sue's help. She reminds me that people took time to organize the event. They booked a room, assembled a panel.

But Sue says something happens once I tell my story. After every event, people hang around and ask me more questions. People never realized things like this happened. They can relate to me. They're appalled, and that's good.

I think one of the reasons Larry took my case was that I'm a white, Midwestern guy. I proved that these things didn't just happen in the ghetto. Plus, I was older. I wasn't a kid who got railroaded. I was college educated, more or less middle class, and have an agricultural background.

One question people always ask me is why I didn't want Schneider and Miller to get the death penalty for what they did to my parents. Society has the right to sequester people who are dangerous. But we have to work to rehabilitate them and make sure everyone is treated humanely. Including the people who killed my parents.

I don't look down on other family victims who feel differently. Those people are hurting. They have tremendous rage and hatred for the people who took their loved one away and completely disrupted their lives.

Prosecutors encourage these people to think they'll find closure if they seek the death penalty for the person who committed the crime. But from what I've heard from people who have lived through this, it doesn't help. Having someone executed brings no more closure than having him sit in prison for the rest of his life.

One of the most unfair things about execution is that the people we eventually kill—years later, in most cases—are very different from the people who committed the crime. They're not in the same mental state. People change. As governor of Texas, George W. Bush murdered a Christian woman when he executed Karla Fay Tucker. She had changed in prison and found God. Stanley "Tookie" Williams, who was executed in California in 2005, made tremendous strides to turn his life around while he was in prison.

But things are changing. There's a lot more debate about the death penalty now. Doctors are refusing to administer the drugs for lethal injections. In large part because of my case, McHenry County has admitted there were problems in the past and created a task force to deal with capital cases before they go to trial.

We can do better as a society than to repay brutality with brutality. If I didn't believe that, I'd be hopelessly hypocritical.

Index